Raving Reviews

"After speaking with Jaime about the Money Funnel System, my finances became a little clearer! I applied it immediately. Since implementation of the system, I am three months ahead of my rent. Car payment is next! If done correctly, the Money Funnel System is a life saver. Simple, but genius. Thank you, Jaime!"

—Lamar "Sir Jankster" Jones
Teacher, Author, and Owner of The Jank Gourmet BBQ Sauce

"I was very moved by Jaime and Cristina's testimony about overcoming the job loss. At the same time, I also learned of a new perspective towards money management. The book is very easy to read, not complicated and will appeal to anybody regardless of educational background. Although lots of people are intimidated by math, the graphics and exhibits make implementing the step-by-step process easy to follow and understand. I am very excited to have *The Money Funnel System* on my bookshelves for the community to benefit from!"

— Yenni Espinoza
City of Penitas – Library Director

"My wife and I already had our own system up and running. After learning about the Money Funnel System, it sparked good discussion and reflection between us. We incorporated the Payments Account and opened an extra account to keep another area of our finances better organized and accounted for. It was a beneficial addition for us!"

—Jon & Safiya Baker
Business Consultant & Pharmacist

The Money Funnel System

The Common Sense Guide to Financial Organization

Jaime Xavier Farias
Cristina Marie Farias

LIGHT SWITCH

lsp

PUBLISHING

The Money Funnel System: The Common Sense Guide to Financial Organization

ISBN: 978-1-7335831-7-6

Library of Congress Control Number: 2019903108

Cover Design & Interior Layout: Ronda Taylor, www.heartworkpublishing.com

LIGHT SWITCH PUBLISHING

McAllen, Texas

themoneyfunnelsystem@gmail.com
www.themoneyfunnelsystem.com

Dedication

While this is not written as a faith-based book, we want to give credit where credit is due. We thank God wholly for the wisdom to apply this system to our life and courage to pursue the vision He gave us for it.

We also dedicate this endeavor to our children: Isaiah Xavier, Emma Marie, Lucy Elizabeth, and Elijah Luke.

Our desire is to leave a legacy of financial wisdom and heart for generosity with you all. We love you each very much!

Contents

Foreword from William Danko

At first, I was reluctant to recommend *The Money Funnel System*. The idea seemed sound, but the manuscript needed refining. Jaime and Cristina worked at it – just as they worked at organizing their finances – and the end result is a solid, accessible, short book that will help many get their financial houses in order.

In an easy to read format, the point is made that one must be organized and disciplined to tame the chaos of the money tornado. Clearly, without the discipline to save and allocate, one will wander aimlessly and never achieve financial peace.

I started my research into wealth in America in 1973. After all these years, there are some truths that never change. One cannot build wealth without knowing how to make money. Once money comes in, the question of how to allocate it must be addressed. Do you spend it all? Do you save? Do you invest for the future? Certainly, there are variations on these basic questions, but the key is to address the spend, save, invest questions in a clear manner, consistent with your values.

Once you master the need to be a consistent saver, you can turn your attention to investing in order to build wealth. Consider the saying: when you are young, you work for money; when you are old, money works for you. If you are to have money work for you through your investments, you must be a saver first. It is as simple as that. The Money Funnel System will get you started in a systematic way and works for ALL income levels!

You can do this!

William D. Danko, Ph.D.
Coauthor of *The Millionaire Next Door,* and
Richer Than A Millionaire ~ A Pathway To True Prosperity

Prologue

You never know how a conversation over coffee with friends will change your life. Sitting down with Andy and Melissa back in December of 2015 altered our financial perspective forever. That little chat over Dave Ramsey's "Financial Peace University" is what propelled us to educate ourselves further on how we could take control of our finances.

We were on a mission: we would be better stewards of the income and opportunities put before us. We would practice wisdom, patience, discipline, and generosity, *purposely* within our finances.

Living in this consumeristic and materialistic society where we are faced with the challenge to keep up with those around us, to always have the "bigger and better"—it is no easy task to place restrictions upon yourself. We have learned over the years to be mindful of what we have and focus less on what we don't. We are thankful for the blessings that have come our way, but we are equally thankful for the hardships and hurdles we've faced because it was surely through those that we grew and saw things more clearly.

We created a financial organization system for our family, and it worked! It worked so well, we wanted to share it with anyone who would listen.

How do we know it worked? Because our bills are paid every month, on time. We have a great credit score because of it, which was a huge help in purchasing our second home. And we got some great perks, like waived set-up fees on utilities because we don't miss payment. But the most important factor is that our marriage is so much better because we don't fight about money.

If that isn't a measure of success, then we don't know what is.

We Just Want to Share

It is important to know that we do not have any degrees in finance nor are we licensed to advise on or sell any financial products. We aren't professional speakers or teachers.

This whole book was born from the realization that we didn't have any control of our money when we did the all-in/all-out, one-account system. That's how many people manage their money, and it creates problems. As you read through the book, you will notice that we are talking to somebody who is currently running all their spending, payments, and savings (if any) out of a single account. People face different circumstances so we touch on various situations that the average and not-so average household faces financially. We certainly haven't addressed all scenarios though. That would be impossible. But we give you the basics of the system so that you can make it work for you.

Some families may have one account at one bank, some may have multiple accounts at one bank, while others are already using multiple accounts at multiple banks. Maybe you will read through the book and simply re-name and designate accounts as we will teach you to do. Maybe you are already running a system that works for you, and that's great, too.

Our wish for you is that by applying the principles of the Money Funnel System you will learn how to run your existing system more efficiently. This may just be a little boost to stay the course, tweak your method, or embark on a complete overhaul. Regardless of what your financial organizational setup currently is, we hope you find nuggets of helpful information and words of encouragement for you to take away. In the end, we feel anybody who reads this book will benefit in one way or another.

To be clear, this is not a "get out of debt" book. There are plenty of authors out there that can teach you exactly what you should do with money. There are trained and licensed financial advisors, and that is their job.

Our intention is to help families get organized with their finances. Once that is accomplished, then the possibilities are endless. If getting out of debt is something you would like to do, this system can definitely help with that. If saving for a vacation, a new car, or more money for retirement is your goal, then this system is a place to start.

We repeat: we won't be telling you what to do with your money. We will, however, be advising you on how you can organize it.

Ideally, you will analyze how you run your finances now, read the book, and then reassess to see if you should make some changes. We figured out a way to not struggle over money anymore. We want you to experience that same freedom.

Our primary goal is to help individuals or families create clarity, control, and efficiency within their finances. Read on if that is your goal as well.

CHAPTER 1

Necessity is the Mother of All Invention

As much as we want every family to take the ideas, advice and concepts taught in this book to heart, we realize that simply will not be the case. Some people don't need to change their financial habits. Some people don't want to change their financial habits. In either case, let's take a minute or two to reflect.

Ask yourself the following questions:

- Do you find yourself wondering where all your money went at the end of the month?
- Do you have financial goals that you'd like to accomplish but don't believe you have the right funds to do it?
- Do you struggle to maintain your monthly budget of expenses and spending?
- Do you feel like you lack control over your finances?
- Do you want to be more generous with your money, but you feel financially inadequate to do so?
- Do you ever miss a monthly payment?
- Do you spend too much money and put your household in trouble because you can't pay a bill?

If you answered "yes" to any one of these questions, then this book is for you. Don't hesitate to dive right in because what you will uncover is a great way to better run your personal finances with clarity, control, and efficiency.

One final question to consider is this: Are you living paycheck to paycheck? More importantly, do you *want* things to stay that way?

If you implement the system we teach in this book, you will be ahead of your payments and not behind them. Making the same money, paying the same bill, on the same date will feel so much different. After reading this book, our hope is that you will ask yourself, "Why didn't I think of this before?"

Our Beginnings

All of us have unique beginnings when it comes to our financial experience and understanding. We first learn how to handle money by watching how our parents work. We grew up in households that had practically opposite ways of thinking and acting about money. One way focused on saving and frugality (which is simply being economical with your money), which we hold fast to in our system. But the other way, a more lackadaisical approach, is also key because it shows that no matter what you learned, or didn't learn, when you were young, it's what you do now that matters.

Jaime's Story

My parents instilled the idea of working hard and saving money in my brother, sister, and me from a very young age. They were both educators who didn't make a lot of money, but they sure did know how to handle it. Their financial habits and practices stuck with me.

I distinctly remember my parents saving spare change for years in order to pay cash for my braces. We packed sandwiches on vacations and ate them for almost every meal, earning my mom her nickname of "sandwich queen." Planning and sacrifice—that was my money foundation.

From the time we were old enough in elementary school, all the way up through high school, my parents encouraged me and my brother to cut yards to earn extra money. It instilled in me an entrepreneurial spirit that is still very much alive today. I have my main job, but also run a side business. All the money my siblings and I earned we got to keep and do with as we pleased. I remember getting those checks and riding to the bank on my bike to deposit them into my account. As I got older, I became a lifeguard and kept cutting yards during high school. I never wanted to spend any of the money. I've always been a natural saver. Some people have even called me "cheap" because of my frugal ways, but I'm okay with that.

Cristina's Story

I, on the other hand, was not necessarily brought up that way. My parents were more laid-back about money. They were less purposeful about saving and spending, and the natural consequence to that was we always felt the weight of relying on the next paycheck. That is not to say they were frivolous spenders, but I guess if I could sum up their perspective on money, it would be "Some days you have it, some days you don't," and "Everything will turn out okay if you just keep working hard."

In fact, to this day, I don't recall a time when we ever really talked about finances in our family. It was clearly something not taught to my parents so they didn't teach it to us. We simply got by on what we had and made the best of situations. My parents were also always willing to help others better their own situations, even if it meant setting themselves back.

While I value the fact that my parents were generous and never raised us to think that more money meant a happier life, I did come to see how the lack of financial savvy did not help me wade the waters of adulthood. I would spend my paycheck until it ran out, and I had to learn lessons the hard way. After accruing over $1,000 in credit card debt in college (of what actually started as a $40 purchase with a few other small purchases), I realized it wasn't fun to be ignorant about money. One of my uncles helped me out by giving me the money to pay off the card. Once that debt was off my back, I never wanted to feel its weight again! I learned that I needed to make careful choices with my income and that credit cards were *not* free money that the nice banks were just handing out.

By the time Jaime and I were married, I'd say we were on the same page ninety-nine percent of the time when it came to financial decisions. This would benefit us years down the road when the rug got pulled out from under us.

Facing Change

We all have a beginning when it comes to setting the course of our financial habits. As we said in the previous section, that beginning does not have to determine the end, so long as we are willing to step in and change it. The financial habits we set forth during our first years of marriage are a testament to that. We were never spending extravagantly, but we were not being wise with our money either. Life has a way of waking you up to your mistakes though.

It was April 10, 2015, when I got a call from my employer that put us in a position we weren't expecting. After a single five-minute phone call, I had gone from an engineer for a large oil field service company to unemployed.

Change. It can be unwanted and unexpected. In our case, it was both. We had two small children (Isaiah, four, and Emma, two), and my wife was four months pregnant with our third child (Lucy). Once I received my last paycheck and severance payment, our income stopped. My wife was a stay-at-home mom so my income was our only income.

Fortunately, we had a small savings account to hold us over. That was all we would have to work with, and we had to make sure we didn't blow it—literally and figuratively! The reality was that we had some money to work with, but we didn't know how long we would have to live off it.

I constantly searched for work. I spent my days applying for various types of jobs and stressing out when I didn't get hired. Days were tough to get through, and there were times I broke down. Being unable to provide for my family is what hurt the most. To supplement some income, I walked up and down the neighborhood with my lawnmower and weed eater looking to cut grass. It was a humbling experience, but I wouldn't change that lesson for the world. When times are tough, we have to get out and do something—anything!

Additionally, we also applied for various types of government aid. After we were repeatedly denied, we realized that relying on the government to help us out when we needed a boost was not an option. Our household needs still had to be met regardless of having no income, so setting some boundaries on our spending was a must.

About three months later, by the grace of God, I came across a job. This job has been more than just an income. It has been a total blessing to our family in so many ways. If I had known that I had to lose a good job to gain a great one, I wouldn't have been so discouraged. As a result of getting laid-off, I have a much greater sense of working hard at my job. I have a new focus, a new drive, and I always strive to put my best foot forward no matter what I do. Sometimes we have to walk through the valleys to get to the mountaintops. God saw us through this time and definitely had a better plan in mind. Once those paychecks started again, we had to be purposed, organized, and more serious about what we did with the income. The importance ranged from how we saved and how we gave to how we spent. It all mattered!

During this dry season, we knew that keeping track of every dollar we had was essential to keeping our heads above water. But this was always a problem for us. It wasn't just during this time of no income; it was when we had income, too. Often, at the end of the month, we would find ourselves asking, "Where did all our money go?" We knew we had a decent amount of money coming in to live off, but we never knew where it all went.

At that time, all our income was going into one account, and out of that same account came all our spending. We spent on bills, on fun shopping, on groceries, on eating out, on unexpected car problems—the list went on. Every time we looked at our account, we never had a real and consistent number in the bank. This all-in/all-out, one-account system was simply not working for us.

Sure we made it, we got by, and technically, we never found ourselves in a dangerous and ever-so-stressful position of "struggling." But were we being good stewards of our resources? No. To be honest, we were being lazy and sloppy.

Where did all our money go was a question that haunted us. We would also ask things like, "I thought we had x amount of dollars?" "Didn't we just get paid?" "How are we going to cover the next bill?" Or the statement that seemed to follow us the most: "Well, let's just transfer from our savings." We tried various money-organization systems. We "tracked" our money (basically just writing down where it all went). We "budgeted" (making a plan for what should be done with the money). Neither worked. We realized you can't win a game by standing by and watching the other team score or by holding on to a game plan you don't implement. Nothing would really change until we got serious, organized, and disciplined.

We needed a system that made the annoying process of paying bills and recurring monthly expenses simple, easy, and organized. We learned that separating our payments from all other spending was key for us to be more responsible with the money we had coming in.

By January of 2016, with the new job well secured, we started following and applying Dave Ramsey's baby steps to work towards getting rid of our mortgage—that was the only debt we had, and we wanted it gone!

But we still needed something to help us with our day-to-day spending. Once we came up with the Money Funnel System, everything changed. We were able to control our spending by purposefully funneling our money into specific accounts and no longer wondered where it went.

Since then, we have not once had to ask ourselves, "Where did all our money go?" Now we know exactly where it all goes! This system will work if you make $20,000 a year or $200,000 a year, income amount doesn't matter. You just need to apply the step-by-step process that we outline in the rest of the book. Customize it where you need to. Put in some discipline to ensure accounts you need to set up are properly funded, and you will soon be enjoying a sense of control and financial freedom most only dream about.

CHAPTER 2

To Be Organized ... or Not:
The Disadvantages of Financial Disorganization

Have you ever stood in one of those money tornado tubes? The thought of free cash can be exciting, but that excitement can soon turn to frustration when you realize that your efforts of catching much money are futile. With the chaos of money flying around you, it is no wonder you don't walk out with gobs of it.

The money tornado tube is a great analogy for the all-in/all-out one-account system, with money flying in and out of that one account. How many of you can relate? With so many transactions happening on a daily/weekly/monthly basis, how can we keep up? From purchasing groceries, filling up the cars with gas, to going out to eat, paying bills, and buying random gifts, the list goes on and on. You are constantly trying to figure out how much money you have and what you have "left" from your paycheck to buy coffee or pay the electric bill.

We've created an illustration that shows the roller coaster ride most people are on when it comes to their money:

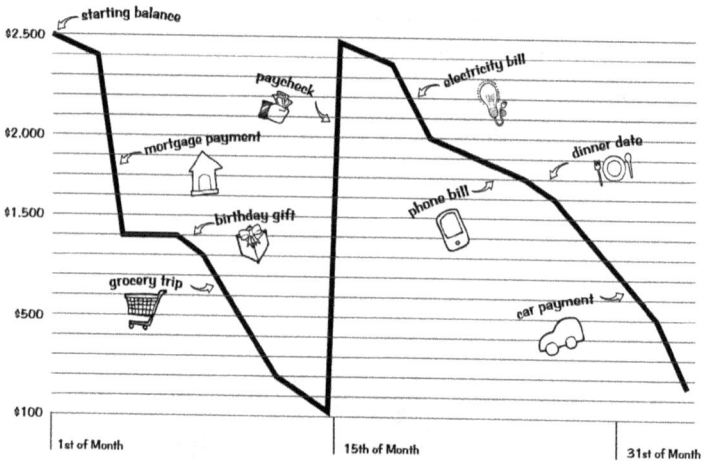

The typical American lives paycheck to paycheck. CNBC reports that seventy-eight percent of all Americans live this way, and given that previous statistics showed seventy-five percent, we can safely say the problem is getting worse.[1] The household above gets paid twice a month, on the first and the fifteenth. You can see their starting balance was $2,500, so that means that their take-home pay is $5,000 per month.

---

1   Jessica Dickler. "Most Americans Live Paycheck to Paycheck." https://www.cnbc.com/2017/08/24/most-americans-live-paycheck-to-paycheck.html.

How does that typically get spent? As you start walking through the month, you can see the household starts depleting the balance. There is a major transaction of $1,200 on the 3rd of the month—that's their mortgage. As the month goes on, they also have more payments and lots of miscellaneous spending running through the account. We are only showing a few but you get the idea. By the fourteenth of the month, the account is almost completely depleted. This family is anxiously anticipating the next $2,500 paycheck because they are nearly out of money.

This is a scary yet all-too normal situation for most people. For one, this family's account almost went to zero before their next paycheck came in and before their car payment was taken out. What if that paycheck hadn't come in? There was nothing stopping that car payment from rearing its ugly head! Was this family even aware they had gotten that close to the line? The last time they looked at the account, there was plenty, but that was before all the small charges for shopping, eating out, and gas, some of which they had accounted for but some not. Then there were the impulse buys—the new purse or upgraded smartphone that they just "had" to have. Because they're not in control of their spending, that is very risky behavior.

Unless you have been in the position of losing a job, you may not understand the risk you are taking by living paycheck to paycheck. We certainly didn't realize the risks we were taking until I was out of a job. People often don't think about their spending habits when they have a steady pay check. They get the next paycheck. They spend it. This is normal. But everyone breathes a sigh of relief when the next check comes in. The vicious cycle continues with no end in sight.

Additionally, many times when you have the all-in/all-out one-account system with a single bank account, your balance is not always an accurate representation. Can you spend every last dollar of that account on a shopping spree? Sure, but then how do you pay your bills? Your payments are coming out of an account that holds the same money you are also casually and randomly spending from.

Don't mix business with pleasure. Then, throw in another person spending from the same account, and you can really get into a mess. Because of the already busy lives many of us lead, it can be quite a difficult task to constantly check your bank account or to find the time to sit down and balance the old checkbook. This is why we fall into financial disorganization, and it's stressful.

Imagine a huge bag of your favorite chips in the center of your table. Open it up and dive in. If you sit there for a while eating away, you have no idea how many chips you have actually consumed. Maybe it was about a quarter of the bag, or maybe it was more like half. Either way, if you really want to count your calories, you will never have a true representation of how many you consumed. Before you know it, you will have eaten far more than half the bag. All you know is that you didn't eat the entire bag and left some chips for the next day. There are two reasons for this: First, our visual perception is that it's a huge bag of chips, so there is plenty. "I can't possibly eat a whole bag of chips!" But because we see so much, we underestimate how quickly we can gobble it all up. Second, once you start...well, you know how it goes. It's quite difficult to practice control when you don't portion things out. You simply can't practice control once you've lost it.

Let's consider the option of going to a buffet dinner versus a restaurant. How many times do you order a second plate at a restaurant? Probably not very often—you eat what is in front of you and leave. Maybe you even bring home some leftovers. Going to a buffet, how many plates do you get? Surely, more than one, and dessert on top of that.

How we handle our money works the same way. When you have your whole check going into a single account while spending and paying bills out of it, you can easily lose track of where your money is going or how much you are actually spending. It may look like you have a nice chunk of money in your account, but once those payments and smaller extra charges go flying out, the balance changes quickly. Also, it may be difficult to control your spending when you see your account right after payday. Using our system, you will have created control over where your money goes by portioning out your money according to your expenses, savings, spending, and income. This is portion control for your finances!

Financial disorganization leads to costly late fees, excessive interest, and unnecessary stress on your household. Not keeping track of your spending and bills leads to frivolous spending, something we hope to cure with this book.

The Race

All of us are in a race every single month. It's the race to get to the end of the month without running out of money and still having paid all our bills. It's all about making ends meet. Some run the race without even breaking a sweat. This may be due to good financial choices or a fabulous income. For others, the race is much harder. This could be due to poor financial choices or even a lack of income. In either case, regardless of the circumstances, the competitors remain the same, each and every entity ready to withdraw or receive that next payment you owe them. You are trying to keep money in your account as fast as they are trying to take it out.

It can be difficult to keep up with all of these competitors. Many times, it can feel like they come out of nowhere. The competitors never get tired and never drop out. Their resources and abilities to keep you behind them can seem overwhelming. Occasionally, they may slow down and let you catch up. The penalties that can also be accrued serve as a setback as well. However, this is not always the case.

How do we come out the winner every time? How do we finish with more money left than what was taken out? It may take a little extra effort prior to the race, but the best way to gain the victory in these monthly races is to give yourself a head start.

By following the Money Funnel System, you give yourself a commanding lead over your competition. If the "making ends meet" race is a three-mile race, wouldn't it be great to start at mile two every month? Imagine finishing the race before the next month even starts!

Have you ever been in a position where a bill is due before your paycheck comes in? We have been there more than we would like to admit. For a short period of time, we were school teachers. When we both brought home a check, we didn't really feel the stress of having to pay bills. The competition we faced was manageable so winning the race every month didn't feel as hard. It wasn't until Cristina quit to come home and take care of Isaiah full-time that running the race required more effort. Jaime's paycheck came once a month on the twenty-fifth. We had to manage the money until the twenty-fifth of the next month. Stretching out that paycheck during those thirty to thirty-one days was a huge challenge, especially during the summer and winter breaks. Having those three months off in the summer was such a blessing, but it also felt like a curse. We were bored at home and wanted to get out and do stuff. This led to various financial mistakes.

Because of the single paycheck and our lack of financial organization, our ability to compete during those months off was weak. By the time the fifteenth of the month came, we were barely scraping by. That next check could not get here soon enough.

CASE STUDY: Jesse needs an advance on his paycheck.

One day, we were having lunch with a friend. During our lunch conversation, Jesse mentioned to us that he was constantly having to get an advance on his paycheck. He had bills coming in quicker than the money, and he was stressed. As lunch continued, we began discussing the Money Funnel System and how it works. After discussing a few things, we figured out how much money he had going out in the form of payments. Jesse gets paid every Friday, so he always counted his third paycheck as his check to pay the mortgage. Consequently, the second check had to stretch out for two weeks. In his eyes, he only gets three paychecks a month (sometimes four depending on the month) because one is already earmarked as his mortgage check.

So for two weeks in the month, the race is a challenge. He struggles, stresses, and has to get an advance on his paycheck every month to cover his lack of financial organization.

Further discussions lead to the realization that he had $5,000 sitting in an account that wasn't getting touched for anything, earning little to no interest.

I suggested he take that money and immediately start the Payments Account, the foundational account we teach in the Money Funnel System. Explaining that with this system, he won't have to worry about paying his bills for this month. That one action ensured his bills will be paid for the entire month, and can immediately begin looking *ahead* to next month's bills instead of constantly having to play catch up.

After a few months, we caught up and discussed how the system was running. His exact quote: "I don't have to get an advance on my paycheck, and I don't stress anymore about paying my bills." He doesn't even realize sometimes he is paying bills. Everything is paid automatically. He is properly funding the account, a very important aspect we will get into later. Life is far less stressful in his household.

Simply by organizing his finances and making a few key decisions, he completely changed his outlook. The race was difficult before, sometimes too much to handle. But now the race is easy. He finishes every time without even breaking a sweat. He didn't need to ask for a raise or get a second job—he just needed to get organized!

CHAPTER 3

Financial Organization with The Money Funnel System

As parents, nothing brings us more peace than when our son's Legos are all strategically placed in their rightful boxes. Batman pieces go inside the Batman box and the race-car pieces go inside the tiny little race-car box. Then when our son goes to open up a box, we know that all the necessary pieces will be there. The best part? He won't be screaming at us asking where his missing toys are. That, my friends, is organizational bliss.

Out of financial disorganization can arise organization. You *can* organize *how* you spend your money. When you do, that same feeling of "Ahh, I know where things are at" is present. It, too, is blissful.

The Advantages of Financial Organization

In Chapter 2, we told you how we searched for various ways to get control of our money, but nothing seemed to work for us. Then one day in October of 2015, a thought came to Jaime while he was driving around.

We had been trying to come up with a way to not only control our spending, but quickly and efficiently pay our bills so Cristina wouldn't have to worry about searching for a bill in the mail, opening it, paying the bill, all while taking care of the kids and handling meals.

In that moment on the road, it just clicked, and Jaime remembers saying to himself, "If we sit down tonight and figure out how much money we need to pay ALL our bills for the month, why don't we designate an account that only our bills will be paid out of? We can set up everything on automatic withdrawal. We can properly fund the account based on our pay cycles with direct deposit, and, *most importantly,* we can place a full month of bills as our starting balance to give us a head start. Everything else that's left will come home, and that's what we will spend." This was the clear solution to making our payments on time and keeping track of our spending!

If you paid attention, there was a very *crucial* step that we implemented. We placed a full month of bills in our Payments Account as our starting balance. In order to accomplish this, we needed to pull funds from somewhere. Thankfully, we had some stocks from Jaime's previous employer that were easily accessible. We cashed those out and immediately started our Payments Account. Then we began feeding the account weekly with the proper amount so that by the time four weekly paychecks came in, we had filled the account again with what was needed for the month.

By the time the end of the month came, we had paid ALL our bills on time smoothly and efficiently and had replenished the account so that we were ready to tackle next month's race with ease.

We then proceeded to set up our monthly recurring payments for automatic withdrawal – the modern-day equivalent of the "envelope system." Now we had a totally separate account for our bills that was continuously being funded. It was great because the payments were set to be automatically withdrawn each month.

The only thing we had to do was check on the account for any erroneous charges. We knew we had the exact amount of money we needed for our payments because they were the only things coming out of the one designated account. The rest of the paycheck was sent to a separate account so we would now know exactly how much money we had left to work with for our savings, spending, or anything else we wanted to financially tackle.

The Money Funnel System was born. Simple, but oh-so effective.

The Hypothetical $5,000

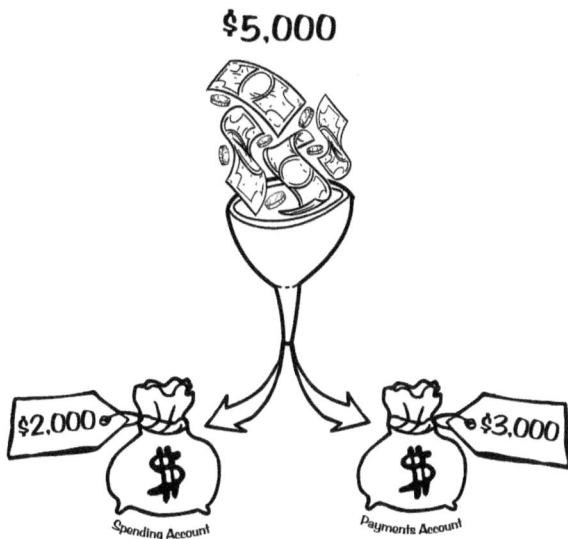

$5,000

$2,000 — Spending Account

$3,000 — Payments Account

Let's take the same $5,000 per month from the hypothetical example we used in the last chapter, the household living paycheck to paycheck. Instead of having it all in one account, spending as you go, what if you applied the Money Funnel System?

The money gets separated into two accounts: the Payments Account and the Spending Account. These are two of the three primary accounts needed to be kept for the Money Funnel System to work. The bills for the month in this example total $3,000. That's what goes into the Payments Account. The remaining $2,000 can be used for spending as you see fit.

When you are looking at your accounts this way, it corrects your flawed visual perception and creates portion control for your spending.

You can see you don't have $5,000 a month to spend; you actually only have $2,000 once all the bills are paid. Furthermore, you have already restricted your spending to $2,000 because you have funneled it into its own account. You can then choose to spend all $2,000 on whatever you need or want because your monthly payments are efficiently being covered and paid out of the other account.

Remember, the goal of the Money Funnel System is to organize your money so you can do more with it, not simply blow through each account. The less money you spend, the more you can put to work on other things. We sincerely recommend keeping a minimum balance in your Spending Account so you can do something more useful with the rest—open up those college funds for your kids, start saving for a new car, set aside money for that vacation you've always wanted. The choices are yours!

Let's pretend this family decided to designate $1,000 for spending and had a goal for the other $1,000. Logging into your bank and checking your account balance instantly shows you how much money you have to work with. You can quickly set a goal for that remaining money, and take action quickly to remove the money from the Spending Account without disrupting your household bills. I had a co-worker state, "I know how much money I have because I balance my checkbook." I agree. When you balance your checkbook, you do know how much money you have, but not instantly.

The Money Funnel System is an instant balance check that can help control your spending. Spending $1,000 in an account that has $5,000 in it is much easier than spending $1,000 in an account that has $1,000. Once you have spent $950, our system will show an account balance of $50. Previously, your account balance would show $4,050, making you feel you have more to spend. Again, it goes back to the flawed visual perception. We perceive lots of extra money, but by the time we start spending, we forget we still have more bills that are yet to be drafted from the account.

This may be a controversial thing to say, but we sincerely believe that much of the cause of this type of living is not simply due to lack of money. It is caused by a lack of contentment with the money that is already earned. We live in a society that is always after the next best thing or trying to keep up with the Joneses. While financial organization is important, we also believe one has to be able to separate "wants" from "needs." Many times we have far more wants than we do needs.

Additionally, we have found that the Money Funnel System works wonders for our marriage. Because we have our finances organized, we hardly ever fight about money. We still have other everyday stresses that come up, but money isn't one of them.

We definitely do not fall into the "wealthy" bracket of Americans, but what money we do bring in, we do right by. We put it where it needs to go and use it wisely. We choose to not live a lavish life but a simple, yet fulfilling life. However, if you want to live the high-life, you can still do so. Spend the money in your Spending Account any way you want—the beauty of the system is you get your bills paid first. Take care of your household first before you spend money. People have it backwards, and the Money Funnel System fixes that.

It's not about how much money you make.

Your key to financial success is how you manage and control your money, including the kind of spending decisions that you make.

The whole reason we wrote this book is to do our part to help families who may or may not be struggling. Regardless of what side of the spectrum you fall on, this system can work for you. Let's take a closer look.

Money Funnel Basics

There's a reason why we call it the "Money Funnel." The dictionary defines the word *funnel* as "a tube or pipe that is wide at the top and narrow at the bottom, used for guiding liquid or powder into a small opening." In this case, the liquid or powder running through the funnel represents your income streams. These income streams pass through the "funnel," and the narrow passage at the bottom leads your income straight into different accounts that are purposefully and intentionally created.

The system can and should be modified and customized to fit the needs of the reader. The sole purpose of this book is to help organize and actually manage your income. When you don't have control over your money, you don't have choices on what you can do with it. Using this system and the order created from it gives you the opportunity to set the vision for what you want to do with your excess money. Go knock out that debt, increase that savings account or save for retirement. When the money is available and you know your bills are paid, your choices increase. Rapidly. We think it's time people understand they can take back control of the money they work so hard for.

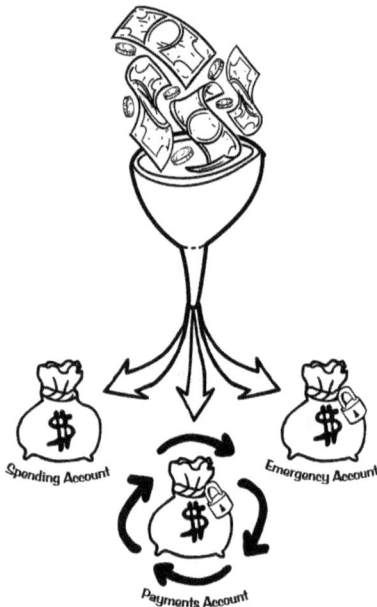

Here is a visual guide as to what the basic Money Funnel System looks like. Specifics of each account will be explained in further detail in Chapters 4, 5, and 6. Throughout the book you will notice the lock and chain image across two of the three accounts. It's locked for a reason. We don't want you to be tempted to touch this money!

We want to make it clear that these accounts in particular should not be tampered with for any reason.

As paychecks come in, they are funneled into their designated accounts. Money gets deposited to your Payments Account from your paycheck, payments are made, money gets deposited, payments are made, and such is the cycle. Hence the circle with arrows.

The rest of your income will be purposefully funneled into the remaining two categories, your Spending Account and Emergency Account. We've talked a little about the Spending Account, but the Emergency Account is important as well. The Spending Account is what you designate for your food, clothes, and any other miscellaneous spending for the month. This may also be the items that fluctuate the most in regards to cost. Gas is an item we also choose to separate, but it's up to you if you want to run gas out of the Spending Account or separate that out into another account, which is what we actually do.

This system is completely customizable to you and your situation. The Emergency Account is an account to be used only for emergencies. Additionally, these accounts can be named differently based on your situation, and you can even open additional accounts as you feel needed. We run our household through six (yes, six), accounts. It may sound like a lot, but it's actually easier than you would think. We have peace knowing that when we spend money, it comes out of the proper account and does not take away from the other needs we have. Tracking it is so easy.

Something to Consider Before Starting

Before we start taking you through the steps, we want to give you a few pointers to keep in mind. It is going to take a little time to fully set up the entire system as we teach. Don't consider it a sprint you are trying to race through. For some it may take longer than others to get started, but it's not about the time it takes. It's just about starting.

Whether you are struggling financially to come up with one month's bills or finding it difficult to make time to set up the automatic payments, don't give up. It could take you one full month or one full year to get your system prepared. Stay the course that is set and work through each step until your system is fully up and running.

A Properly Funded Account

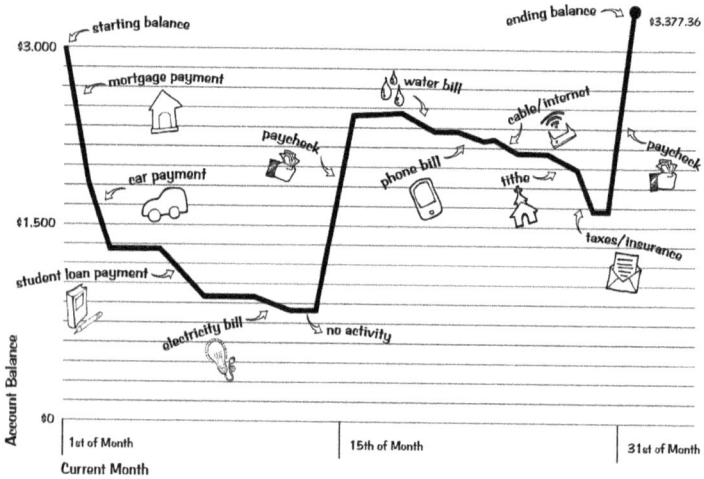

When your accounts are properly funded, you have a wonderful peace of mind. We cannot stress this enough. In the exhibit above, this family has stayed the course and has their Payments Account properly funded with a full month of bills as their starting balance. In this case, that was $3,000. This graph is showing the starting balance, ending balance and walks you through the activity taking place in the account throughout the month.

Let's discuss some key points about what is happening.

First, as we stated earlier, it's important to stress that there are two primary activities occurring simultaneously. You are paying the current month's bills while funding the account for next month's payments, hence the spikes on the fifteenth and the first for $1,500 each—a total of $3,000.

Next, even if your account nears close to zero, with accurate budgeting you can be assured that you will not be overdrawn. By the time the end of the month arrives, the balance in the account is slightly higher than it was when the month started ($3,377.36 vs $3,000). This is $377.36 more than what was in there when the previous month started. This gives you a sneak-peak at what is to come in the next chapter. We recommend overestimating your projected payments. It doesn't have to be much. The results are more money to ensure the account over time won't be depleted. This money stays in the account and gets pushed forward to the next month. You actually have a Payments Account with a balance that is growing as time progresses. This extra money can also be part of the savings aspect of this account, which could be your insurance or tax bills that are due at a later date.

Something worth noting about the graph is the fact that there are periods of no activity. Because you are only paying bills out of this account, there aren't many transactions taking place. If you have five bills and get paid twice a month, you will have a total of seven transactions in this account. That's it. Additionally, you can look at your yearly bank statement and easily digest critical information you may want to analyze.

Now your bills are playing catch up to you, instead of you playing catch up to your bills. You can sit back while your account is being funded, and the bills are efficiently getting paid.

We know to some this may seem like a lot of work and a lot of effort. But consider this. It takes more work to stay afloat and survive in turbulent waters when you don't have a life vest on. It takes little work and effort to slip it on prior to setting out to sea. Put on your life-vest now before you hit turbulent waters. It is unknown how long you will be able to stay afloat without it.

By placing yourself one month ahead, or more, in your Payments Account, you have put on your life vest for when waters in life should get a little turbulent and you need that extra help to stay afloat. We can all enjoy the open water more when wearing one because we have that extra protection. Should the unforeseen happen, we know we won't go under.

CASE STUDY: Rachel Wants to Move Out on Her Own

Rachel is a twenty-two-year old who works full-time as a school teacher. She has always struggled with handling money and unfortunately lives paycheck to paycheck. She has a decent income, but has no idea where her money goes by the end of the month. She has always wanted to move out of her parents' house but worries about having to pay her own bills. In order to help make her feel comfortable about moving out, we wanted to help her create a system that would control her spending and ensure that her bills were paid every month on time, without stress or worry. The basic Money Funnel System works great for Rachel because she now has more clarity and control of the money she brings in.

When we sat down with Rachel and wrote out her bills (rent, electricity, cable, internet), we figured out she needed $850 per month to stay in her apartment. That did not include groceries or gas because she chose to run that out of her Spending Account.

Fortunately for Rachel, she was getting a $1,500 tax return in the mail. Rather than spending that money at the mall or going on a trip, we advised her to take at least $850 and immediately open her Payments Account with it. She actually chose to take $1,000 and used that as her starting balance and used the remaining $500 for her deposit to move into an apartment. She chose to set up an automatic bank draft on her electricity, cable, and internet. When her rent was due, she wrote a check and dropped it off with the landlord on the first of every month.

Being a teacher, she gets one paycheck a month and it comes on the twenty-fifth. She got with her payroll office to split her check. She sends $850 per paycheck to her Payments Account, and the rest is deposited into her Spending Account. Now that she can see what is left for spending, she is designating $250 per paycheck and placing it in her Emergency Account until it gets up to three months of expenses, $2,500 in her case.

If she works summer school or does tutoring on the side, that will only speed up the process and get Rachel where she wants to be financially. She has clarity and control and is no longer living paycheck to paycheck. By organizing her finances and using the Money Funnel System, she now feels comfortable knowing she can make it on her own. She no longer relies on her parents for financial security. She is independent and ready to take on the world.

CHAPTER 4

Setting Up the Payments Account

The Payments Account is the foundational account of this system. It's what guarantees the bills are paid, and it is the account that you cannot touch for any reason other than what it's supposed to be used for.

Properly funded, the Payments Account will smoothly and efficiently run your household obligations for the month.

The following is our step-by-step process for setting up this account. Once implemented and fully working as designed, it's a beautiful thing to sit back and watch it work.

STEP 1: Estimate Your Monthly Income

This step is simple. You need to account for all of the money that you will be running through your funnel (the arrows in our exhibit above). These arrows represent your total income for the month. For most people, it's one or two paychecks from an employer, but for others they could have additional streams of income flowing in.

Grab your last paystub and look at how much the check is. If that paycheck comes in twice a month, multiply it times two. If that paycheck comes in once a month, you are done. If it comes in once a week, then multiply it by four (or five depending on the month). You get the idea. Do the same for any other paycheck that you may be considering as part of your total monthly income (say a check from your spouse or a second job). Come up with a grand total of what your monthly income will be. This will be the first number needed to begin setting up your Payments Account.

- If you're single, you'll just figure it from your own paychecks.
- If there is more than one income in the household, then both need to be added together.
- If you're self-employed, it's a little harder because you don't get a steady paycheck. However, you can estimate how much money you're earning by taking an average of your bank statement for the past six or twelve months.
- If your income fluctuates because you work hourly or work off commission, this step requires a little more work. How do you estimate when income is unpredictable? Try your best to look at a six-to-twelve month time frame. Determine what your lowest paycheck over that time period was and use that as a start. Any time you earn more than your projected amount, simply determine what you want to do with it from there.

Whatever the case may be, if you know how much income is coming into the Money Funnel, it is you or you and your significant other's responsibility to designate how much money goes into each individual account.

Keep in mind, that although we are starting with your income, it is not the end all be all to this system. We are simply trying to gauge what we are working with.

STEP 2: Estimate your payments (your recurring monthly expenses)

Once you know how much money is coming in, you need to determine how much is going out on a monthly basis.

Remember, the goal of this account is to estimate and run your household expenses for the entire month. In order to tackle this step properly, you need to determine what monthly payments will be made. This is a very important step in the process because you must ensure you properly estimate your Payments Account. Underestimating this account can lead to overdraft charges over time.

We suggest looking at the following types of bills to be included in your Payments Account:

- Mortgage
- Electricity
- Water
- Cable/internet
- Phone bill
- Donations/tithe
- Car payment
- School loans

Here are a few other items to consider including in your Payments Account that are not necessarily basic essentials. They are, however, monthly repeated withdrawals that just make life easier when you account for them in advance:

- Health/dental insurance
- Vehicle insurance
- Home insurance (if it's not included in escrow or you have paid off your house)
- ESAs (or any other type of college saving account)
- Life insurance
- City/county taxes
- Tuition

Some payments are the same each month and don't change. Some of them fluctuate. You may even have a bill that occurs every six months, like your car or home insurance. Or you may have a bill due at the end of the year, like your city and county taxes. If coming up with this large chunk can be difficult, we recommend taking the estimated total needed, dividing it out by the number of months it covers (like car insurance that's paid every six months) and include the monthly expense in your Payments Account. The money you need to pay that larger bill will slowly get funded over time. It will sit in this account—so be sure not to spend it. When the bill comes due, you write a check and pay the bill. Done.

The only activity you should see out of this account is what you have budgeted to be withdrawn.

For payments that do not fluctuate, like a mortgage or car payment, slightly overestimate the amount you need. We mentioned this in the previous chapter, and we have found it to be an extra little bit of peace of mind. In our household, a bill that is $44.29 becomes $50, because we always round up at least $5. You can choose to do more, or you can choose to budget that exact amount. It's really up to you. The reason we choose to overestimate is that the leftover money that is not spent ($5.71 in my previous example) will stay in this account and turn into $68.52 over the course of a year ($5.71 x 12). It's a way to provide a little cushion in the account should you need a little extra for other bills that do fluctuate. The more you overestimate, the further ahead you will get over time.

For payments that do fluctuate, like a water or electricity bill, we have chosen to do the following. We looked at that particular bill and found out how much we paid in a worst-case scenario. In our household, the worst-case scenario for electricity is $150.00, which is in December when it's cold. We have a very modest home so there is not a lot of space that needs to be warmed, but since our windows are old and single-paned, air escapes and the heater is constantly running. As we write this book, our average electricity bill for the entire year (January through August) has been $107.97. We have not reached the budgeted amount of $150.00, but as you can see, we are prepared should the bill be higher than expected in December. This account continues to grow. Again, it's all about preparing for the worst and giving yourself that cushion.

Projecting Your Payments Account Form

Here is the form we use to figure out how much we need to fund our Payments Account. It's simple to follow and it allows you to keep track of your bills.

Notice the table has three columns (Name of Bill, Amount and Due Date). We would suggest you place them in the order they are drafted out of your account (or due date) for easier tracking. As bills come due, you can walk down the list until you get to the end of the month. Additionally, you can quickly see how much gets drafted out on a weekly basis, bi-weekly, etc. should you like to know that information.

Projecting Your "Payments Account"		
NAME OF BILL	AMOUNT	BILL DUE DATE
TOTAL		

You can use the form above to list out each and every payment you need to pay for that month, including bills due in six or twelve months. If you need more space, you can recreate this using your "tables" function on your computer or by using a notepad.

Once you have written this down for each bill and come up with a total amount that is needed to fund the Payments Account, you are ready to move to the next step.

Below is an example of what we are talking about.

Just to clarify, the "Insurance" and "Taxes" items of $130 and $170 are monthly projections that will not actually be paid each month. The designated insurance money will build in the account for six months. At the end of six months, the insurance payment will amount to $780 which will cover the cost of the bill when it arrives. Similarly, the designated tax money will build over time and be ready to withdraw when the tax bill comes due at the end of the year.

Projecting Payments		
NAME OF BILL	AMOUNT	BILL DUE DATE
Mortgage	$ 1,200.00	01/03/18
Car Payment	$ 350.00	01/07/18
Student Loan Payment	$ 250.00	01/10/18
Electricity	$ 150.00	01/12/18
Water	$ 75.00	01/23/18
Cell Phone	$ 75.00	01/25/18
Cable/Internet	$ 100.00	01/27/18
Tithe	$ 500.00	01/29/18
Insurance	$ 130.00	Every 6 months
Taxes	$ 170.00	Every 12 months
TOTAL	**$ 3,000.00**	

It's Your Turn

Now it's time for you to figure out how much money should be funneled into your Payments Account.

Projecting Your "Payments Account"		
NAME OF BILL	AMOUNT	BILL DUE DATE
TOTAL		

Tithe/Donations/Charitable Giving

One item we also include in our Payments Account is our tithe. As Christians, this is something we believe in and want to hold ourselves accountable to doing. For others this important act may be done in the form of a donation to a favorite organization or charity. While we don't consider charitable giving an actual bill, we do count it as a monthly recurring investment that absolutely needs to be paid.

We help ourselves be consistent with this calling by placing the payment as a line item in our spreadsheet. The reason why giving out of this account is better than paying out of your Spending Account is the same as with all your other important payments. It can be too easily shrugged off. It's easy to look at giving as an "extra," but for us we believe it's primary. We like to think that we can't afford **not** to tithe so we put it in the account with our non-negotiable payments. It would be easy to spend that money on a new pair of shoes rather than write that check to your church or the charity you support.

This was our problem. We spent our tithe money all the time. Now we wait until the end of the month when the Payments Account is fully funded. Our church has an automatic bank draft available so at the end of the month our tithe is ready to be withdrawn. If your church or charity doesn't have that option, you can still write out a check without feeling any strain, just the joy of giving.

The church benefits because we now don't miss a tithe, but we have benefited more because we are giving back to an organization that plays a vital role in our lives. Since your charitable giving is tied into your payments, there is no turning back. Your charitable giving becomes set and you are now more accountable for it.

STEP 3: Making Your Payments Account an Independent Account

This step is going to vary based on what accounts you are currently using. We stated this earlier in the book but it's important to state it again. Some may have one account at one bank. Some may have multiple accounts at one bank, while others are already using multiple accounts at multiple banks. We do not have time to address each individual situation in this book. It may be that you simply need to identify one account as your Payments Account and decide that it is locked. You can't access the money except for its designated purpose.

You need to read through this step and decide for yourself how to fully implement what we are trying to accomplish according to what fits your current situation.

In order to move forward we are going to assume that you only have one checking account and nothing else. With that being said, we are going to recommend opening a checking account at a separate bank from where you normally bank. Make sure to find out if any restrictions exist on the account that you open. This step is a simple one. Decide what bank you want to deal with and go from there. It is best if the account allows for direct deposit and automatic bank draft, but it is not required.

Now, if you really don't want to open an account at another bank or simply don't have access to a second bank, that's not a problem. You are welcome to run all of the accounts we will be discussing out of the one bank. That's okay. You are just going to have to be more responsible and disciplined, as we are going to explain.

Lock and Chain

The reason why you want to consider your Payments Account locked is so you don't spend it.

If you are going to run all your accounts out of the same bank, you will need to be extra diligent about not touching the Payments Account. This is why we recommend you use separate banks for your payment and spending accounts. The temptation to transfer money to your Spending Account will always be there if the accounts are in the same bank.

The money in your Payments Account is designated for running the household and for *nothing else*. The arrows below the lock and chain illustrate deposits and withdrawals, the only activity in this account. You pay the bill, money gets deposited, pay another bill, pay another bill, money gets deposited, and such is the continuous cycle every month.

Additionally, when we log into the bank and look at the balance in the Spending Account, we don't want to look at this account and think we have money in there that we can transfer over or have access to. Opening the Payments Account at a separate bank also makes it much harder for you to withdraw money.

In our household Cristina carries the debit card for the Payments Account. It's used to deposit checks at the ATM or to withdraw money to pay a cash bill for childcare (when we had the kids in day care). Nothing else.

This is one of those things where you just have to be responsible and not use the Payments Account for any miscellaneous transactions. If keeping it in an easily accessible place is going to be too tempting for you, then you should keep it in a safe and secure place at home, or don't have one at all.

If you choose to dip into this account for the sole purpose of buying a new designer purse or bigger tires for your truck, then your issue is not organization. It's spending control.

Recently in a coaching session, the couple that we met with called this account a "non-negotiable" account. The husband stated that the wife likes to be generous at times, which sometimes creates conflict in the household. Our response was that if you want to be generous, great! But you should not take money from this account. You should be generous from your Spending Account. Remember, this account runs the household for the month. It really should not be touched for any reason.

Now that you have the account, let's get it working for you.

STEP 4: Find Your Starting Balance

We do not recommend setting up a Payments Account and then immediately start automatically withdrawing bills. This may lead to overdraft charges.

Rather, our goal is to have you open the Payments Account with a starting balance equal to one month's worth of bills. If you determined in Step 2 that you need $3,000 a month to pay your bills, then either open an account with $3,000 or work hard to build up the account so that you have the one month ahead.

For some this step is easy. They may have company stocks they can cash out, a tax return coming, Christmas bonus or some combination of all of them. Maybe you have additional money sitting stagnant in a savings account, earning practically no interest. Consider doing something more valuable with it and start your Payments Account. Whatever the case may be, consider using this extra money to immediately fund your Payments Account. If you already have the money just sitting around, you might as well put it to good use.

We would not recommend cashing out retirement to fund this account. Depending on your age and how the money is allocated, penalties may be associated with that transaction.

For others this step is hard. Presenting this system to many different people in various situations, they often ask the question, "How can I do this if I have no money left after bills are paid?" One problem is they have more money going out than they have coming in. They are barely making it and have lost hope of ever getting ahead. Another problem people face, which is the whole point of this book, is a lack of organization and control over their finances. Though we believe in the simplicity of this system, we know the reality is that most people struggle and don't have the money sitting around to start their Payments Account right away.

As we stated earlier, this is not a "get out of debt" book. Our goal is to help create a financial organization system for the reader. If you have no room in your budget and can't figure out why you can't make it, then that's where Dave Ramsey and others can help you navigate that situation. For example, if you have a $25,000 car and you make $40,000 a year, that's a problem. You have more than fifty percent of your annual income tied up in a car. If you have a $25,000 car and you make $100,000 a year, that's not your problem. If you have a $1,500 mortgage and you bring home $3,000 a month, there is your problem. You have fifty percent of your paycheck tied up in a house payment. Those are the situations we don't address in this book, but they do need to carefully be analyzed to determine what the problem is.

We have a recently divorced friend. She is a teacher and has a $3,000 paycheck coming in per month, plus some child support. She has a $1,500 mortgage as well as a $325 car payment. With those numbers she is always going to find herself struggling to stay ahead. After she pays her bills, buys groceries and gas for her car, that's it. No money left.

After introducing her to the Money Funnel System and brainstorming a bit, she recognized where she was and what she needed to do in order to start her Payments Account. She started up her side business again, sold her house, and rented something else more affordable. She told us at that time, "I want to be one of your success stories!" She saw the light at the end of the tunnel and wasn't afraid to enter it.

Everyone is in their own unique situation and will have to make their setup choices accordingly. Truthfully, the problem many times is that people simply don't want to sacrifice now to flourish later. Is that the case one hundred percent of the time? No. We have talked to many people who have bills knocking at their door as they support their kids through college. Somebody loses a spouse while car problems and home repairs keep piling up. We get it. That's where people must review their own situation, and look long and hard about what can be done to either cut lifestyle expenses or increase income for a short period of time.

It may take a family twelve months or more to save up enough money to fund the Payments Account. So what! Be intentional, be proactive, and be patient. This step may take time, but know that a little sacrifice will be worth it in the end. As the old saying goes, "Where there's a will, there's a way!"

When your Payments Account is fully up and running, you will have two primary activities occurring simultaneously. You will be paying the current month's bills while funding the account for next month's payments.

Remember, you have already deposited the money for this month's bills into the account. As a result you will no longer be living paycheck to paycheck. Now your next paycheck will start funding next month's bills, as this month's bills are already taken care of.

STEP 5: Method of Payment

Once you have the account funded, you need to figure out how you are going to pay your bills.

How you pay your bills is completely dependent on how you choose to manage this account, thus we are going to present different options to consider. Some people prefer to pay everything on automatic bank draft. If your bank offers online bill pay and you choose to manage the account using that method, great. Our suggestion is to utilize automatic bank draft through each company that offers it.

Some would rather write checks while others prefer to pay with cash. Each of these options is fine, as long as your bills are paid.

Most if not all companies make automatic bank draft available to the customer. It takes the work out of having to physically write the check or even pay your bills online.

If you choose automatic bank draft, you are going to need to call each company and give them the routing and account number from your Payments Account.

They will also ask you for a date to draft the money from the account. You can pick the actual due date or a few days before. That's up to you. Once you give them those two pieces of information, you are good to go.

Actually, there are many companies now that give you the option of setting this up online also. (See image on following page).

This is just a sample of the automatic bank draft setup page from one of the companies we pay every month.

We are aware that some people may have their reservations about this modern way of making payments. As we mentioned before, you have the option of how you choose to pay the bill. Our main reason for using and recommending automatic bank draft is to avoid overlooking a bill that arrives in the mail. This was one of the constant challenges we faced while dealing with the hustle and bustle

Pay by Bank Draft

Account Type

Routing Number

Re-Enter

Bank Account Number

Re-Enter

Billing Address

Name*

Address*

City*

State*

Zip*

Payment Mode

⊙ Pay now & set as recurring to pay future bills automatically

☐ Update generated bills are recurring for auto draft

☐ Make one-time payment

Authorize

☐ Authorize Payment

Please note that payment will be credited to your account only after we receive an approval from your Bank authorizing the charges. This process may take up to 2 business days. If payment is declined, you may incur late charges depending on the due date on your invoice, a returned check fee of up to $30 and possible service interruption.

Submit Payment   **Cancel**

of life. With so much going on, checking the mail always seemed to be put on the back burner.

Cristina will tell you that it's not fun having your utilities cut off because you forgot to pay a bill. It was 2013. We decided that she should stay at home with our kids, and Cristina was still new to that role. She was trying to balance the workload in the home, take care of our two young children, and stay on top of paying bills. Somehow the water bill got missed for a few months. Since we had no sure way of keeping track of when the bills were paid, it was easy to miss.

What ended up happening was what any busy parent would not want—our water got cut off. First of all, Cristina cried and felt like a horribly irresponsible adult. It's not like we didn't have the money to pay the bill. We just simply forgot about it. Secondly, it turned into a huge inconvenience not only because we didn't have water in our home, but because she had to head down to the city utilities office to rectify the situation. With two kids in tow, it really was not what she wanted to have to do.

Sadly, this was not the only time we dealt with a forgotten bill. It took more than one overdraft charge, late fee, or apologetic call to the company explaining again how "I didn't see the bill" to make us realize that something had to change. With the Money Funnel System, it takes all the weight and burden of paying bills off her shoulders.

With automatic bank draft set up, it ensures that the bills get paid even if you miss the bill or don't open the mail. The cherry on top is pretty awesome. We never pay a late fee, and we never have to worry about having our utilities being cut off.

Does this picture below look familiar? I'm sure there is a bill somewhere in this pile! Do yourself a favor and be efficient with your time and money. Both are too valuable to waste.

Now it's time to start funding your Payments Account based on your pay cycle, which we will explain in Chapter 7.

In Step 2, we asked you to complete your chart that lists out your bills. If you've not done that step, now is the time to do it.

To give you a good illustration to follow, we're using the same chart we used as an example above. It is a snapshot of the first day of the month before any activity has taken place in the Payments Account:

Projecting Payments		
NAME OF BILL	AMOUNT	BILL DUE DATE
Mortgage	$ 1,200.00	01/03/18
Car Payment	$ 350.00	01/07/18
Student Loan Payment	$ 250.00	01/10/18
Electricity	$ 150.00	01/12/18
Water	$ 75.00	01/23/18
Cell Phone	$ 75.00	01/25/18
Cable/Internet	$ 100.00	01/27/18
Tithe	$ 500.00	01/29/18
Insurance	$ 130.00	Every 6 months
Taxes	$ 170.00	Every 12 months
TOTAL	**$ 3,000.00**	

Remember all of these amounts have been fluffed slightly. Not all of the amounts above are what will actually be drafted. Some bills will be exactly what was projected, while others will be less. If your actual payment was more than what was projected, then over time some adjustments may need to take place.

The image on the following page is a snapshot on the last day of the month showing the actual payment amounts that got drafted. Once the bill gets drafted, we go into our spreadsheet and highlight the cell in green and start moving down the spreadsheet until the entire month is complete.

We started with a budget of $3,000 and ended with actual payments that totaled $2,922.64. That leaves us with an extra $77.36 that will be rolled over into next month and not touched ($377.36 if you include the savings aspect of the account).

Actual Payments		
NAME OF BILL	AMOUNT	BILL DUE DATE
Mortgage	$ 1,200.00	01/03/18
Car Payment	$ 350.00	01/07/18
Student Loan Payment	$ 250.00	01/10/18
Electricity	$ 99.78	01/12/18
Water	$ 52.35	01/23/18
Cell Phone	$ 74.84	01/25/18
Cable/Internet	$ 95.67	01/27/18
Tithe	$ 500.00	01/29/18
Insurance	$ 130.00	Every 6 months
Taxes	$ 170.00	Every 12 months
TOTAL	**$ 2,922.64**	

Are you tired of having to pay bills due this month with the same paycheck you are receiving this month? That stress is something that *can* be handled. It may take some time and more than a little discipline to get this Payments Account funded and working properly, but the relief you feel when it's on automatic can't be overstated.

CASE STUDY: Daniel's System for his Elderly Parents

All of us eventually face the reality of our parents getting older and not being able to take care of themselves. For some whose parents live close, the stress and worry can be alleviated slightly in knowing they are close. If they need something, are in an emergency, or for whatever reason are in danger, you are close and can be there to help in any way you can. For others this challenging circumstance gets much more difficult when the parents are living out of town or in another state. Being there at the drop of a dime is impossible. Getting on a flight or driving four hours in a car is much more difficult and time consuming. Yes, some things can be handled on the phone, but for the most part your parents are on their own most of the time.

Income Stream

For Daniel's parents, this is exactly the reality he is facing. To make things worse, his mother suffers from Alzheimer's and his father is disabled. Setting up the basic Money Funnel System was perfect for his parents' situation. See, Daniel's parents were always spending too much money. As soon as their Social Security/Disability checks would get direct deposited, the money would too quickly get spent. As a result he was never fully aware if they were going to be able to pay their rent, water, and electricity every single month. Taking that phone call from his parents asking for money came at least every other month. Daniel doesn't have any extra room in his budget for these unexpected expenses, so we needed to figure something out.

We explained that the bills needed to get separated out from the spending, and until that is accomplished the problem is going to continue. After the Money Funnel System is up and running, his parents could technically wipe out their checking account of any money, and he could ensure that they still efficiently paid electricity, water and their rent. The "lock and chain" around the Payments Account is critical in this situation.

Daniel had to sit his parents down and explain what was going to happen because things could not continue as they were going. This was the only option and his parents reluctantly agreed to give it a try.

There was a glitch that made things a little tricky, and that was the fact that you can't send your Social Security/Disability checks into multiple accounts. One hundred percent of the money must get deposited into one account. This was the tricky part that Daniel had to navigate.

In order to ensure that the designated bills money got deposited into the Payments Account, Daniel needed to give himself access to the account in order to be able to transfer the proper amount of money to the Payments Account once a month. A meeting with the branch manager was scheduled, so he and his parents could explain the situation, and he was allowed access to the account via the internet.

The Money Funnel System works, and in this case worked beautifully for Daniel and his parents. Daniel can sleep better at night knowing that his parents are paying their bills every month on time.

CHAPTER 5

The Emergency Account

Throughout the book we've mostly been talking about the Payments Account and the Spending Account. The Payments Account, properly funded, is what makes this system work so well. The spending part is *fun*, especially when you know you're not taking money away from your household expenses. We have also mentioned the importance of an Emergency Account.

Even though everyone wants to know how much they can spend worry-free every month, it's important to actually make sure that you have your Emergency Account set up next. The reason is simple. Just as it's easy to spend money on the fun stuff and not the bills, it's even easier to justify not setting money aside.

According to a recent survey, sixty-five percent of all Americans do not save any money.[2] If an emergency happens and someone has to go to the hospital or if something on the car breaks down, what do you do?

When I lost my job, as we mentioned in the beginning of the book, I was working as an engineer in the oil field. The oil field market is up and down. It was like a roller-coaster ride every single day. There were times when the company was super busy and other days when there was nothing to do. We looked ahead and saw storm clouds on the horizon, and although the call was a shocker, we weren't surprised when I got laid off. When a company decides to make a change, they don't call you and ask your advice. They make

---

2   Emmie Martin. 65% of Americans Save Little Or Nothing and could end up struggling in retirement. Mar 15, 2018. https://www.cnbc.com/2018/03/15/bankrate-65-percent-of-ameri-cans-save-little-or-nothing.html. Accessed Dec 14, 2018.

their decision, and you have to deal with it. We made it through this three-month layoff because we had some money tucked away. That experience would have been *far* different if we didn't have any savings.

It taught us the value of having an Emergency Account. You're saving for that inevitable rainy day. It adds a layer of security that can give you even more peace of mind about your finances.

An Umbrella When It Rains

First and most importantly, you will notice we have a lock and chain around the Emergency Account just as we do on the Payments Account. This account is specifically designed as the title says—emergencies only. This money is to be used to cover those unexpected expenses we all know are going to happen. Don't those unexpected expenses always happen at the worst time? It's like getting caught in the rain without an umbrella. Having an account that can turn an emergency into an inconvenience feels really good, trust me.

For example, our son Isaiah broke his arm at school, and we had to cover hospital/doctor visits. We used our Emergency Account to cover those expenses, so it didn't take away from our household bills. Our household didn't skip a beat. Our bills were getting paid efficiently and on time, so we didn't have to worry about keeping the lights on or paying the water bill. We could focus on the emergency we had directly in front of us, and that's it. It was a small speed bump that we drove over with ease because of the Money Funnel System and how it's designed to work.

The basic Money Funnel System always has an Emergency Account. It will be funded when you get disciplined about your spending. Let's take the hypothetical $5,000 a month income. We know $3,000 goes to paying bills. The other $2,000 could be split in half, with $1,000 designated for spending and the other $1,000 deposited into a savings account. Over a period of time, you could really build up the account balance in the Emergency Account up to where you feel comfortable. You want to have some money in there to cover emergencies, and, yes, you will have emergencies.

Account Transactions

The activity in this account is going to be sporadic so opening a savings account should be sufficient. The purpose of this account is to tackle those emergencies we are never expecting. Below are examples of the types of emergencies you may encounter:

- Transmission goes out in your car
- Losing your job
- Government shutdown
- Water heater replacement
- Air condition breaks down
- You come down with the flu
- Flooding from a bad storm

These are just a few examples of the types of emergencies you may encounter. Some are going to be huge bills that you may not be able to fully cover, while others are manageable and can easily be taken care of. How much money should be in this account? Let's discuss.

Target Balance

There are a few things to consider when trying to decide how much money should be in this account. There are experts out there, like Dave Ramsey, who would say place three to six months of household expenses in the account. In Chapter 4 we discussed how you should estimate how much money you should send to your Payments Account monthly. Using Dave Ramsey's guide, you would then get that balance and multiply it by three or by six and use this as a target.

For example, if you figured out you needed $3,000 per month for your Payments Account, then you would multiply that by three

($3,000 x 3 months = $9,000) or six ($3,000 x 6 months = $18,000). That's a lot of money. We get that.

At this point you have to decide what emergency balance you feel comfortable with. In our account we have a target goal of $12,000, but that's us. Yours may be less, it may be more. The choice is yours.

There are some things you can consider when trying to decide your target balance. Is your job volatile? Do you see some big change coming in the next year or two? Is your spouse quitting his/her job to come home and take care of the kids? Are you self-employed? If you answered yes to any of these questions, then you probably want to be on the six-month side of the equation.

If you work a very stable job and don't foresee change on the horizon, then maybe you can be on the three-month side of the equation. Only you, the reader, can look around and analyze the volatility of your income.

Once you have an idea of what to shoot for, let's discuss where the money should be stored.

Account Location

First and most importantly, you need to have quick access to this money. You don't want to drive to the bank two hours away in order to have access. The money needs to be available to you at a moment's notice so you can tackle whatever situation you may encounter. Our Emergency Account is at a bank located two miles from our house. We can get in the car and quickly access the money. It doesn't take much time.

We are going to recommend opening this savings account, your Emergency Account, at the same bank where you have your Payments Account. If you recall in Chapter 4/Step 3 we recommended restricting access to your Payments Account. Same goes with the Emergency Account. We don't want you to have access to this money unless you need it. You may think that a new couch for the living room is an emergency, but it's not. If you can imagine, now we have a lock and chain around the entire bank! The money sitting in this bank serves two specific purposes. It runs your household for the month, and it covers those unexpected emergencies. Nothing else.

Which Account Funds First?

In Chapter 4 we recommended starting your Payments Account with one month's worth of bills. You may be asking yourself, "Which account am I supposed to properly fund first?"

The order in which we introduce the accounts is the order they should be tackled. Remember, the Money Funnel System teaches you to take care of your household first before spending any money. We are going to recommend fully building up the proper balance in your Payments Account before shifting your focus to the Emergency Account. If an emergency does come, you can always pause and tackle the emergency with the money you are using to build up your Payments Account.

We know that sometimes it's hard to make ends meet. But we also know how nice it was to have money when we needed it. We can tell you it's worth the sacrifice you make to tuck some money away. Let's say you can only put $50 a month away. That's fine. You'll start seeing the balance rise, and that may be motivation to find ways to save even more. Maybe take one less trip to the coffee shop every week or bring lunch from home. You will be amazed how much money you can save by doing even those small things.

Refill the Balance

Once you have achieved the proper balance in your Emergency Account, it will only be a matter of time before you must withdraw money. Let's say you've funded your Emergency Account to your desired limit. You may not be currently sending any money to the Emergency Account, but once that balance takes a hit, it's time to refill as quickly as possible.

You don't want to deplete the account and leave it with little or even no money available. You want to be rebuilding the account to its target balance so you're ready for the next inevitable mishap that will come your way. Imagine suffering a severe laceration while swimming out in the ocean. Rather than getting yourself to safety immediately, you slowly make your way back to shore. But then out of nowhere a shark comes and attacks you.

That next emergency will come out of nowhere, so be ready!

Our account took a hit with those unexpected medical expenses incurred by Isaiah's broken arm, but instead of just letting the account sit as is, we have cut our spending habits down so that we can build up the Emergency Account again. We didn't have to worry about money when Isaiah broke his arm, and we don't want to have to fret when the next emergency happens. We shifted our focus back to the Emergency Account and replenished it back to its target balance.

The best advice we can give you is to limit your spending once again and be ready to tackle the next hurdle.

Automate the Process if Possible

For those of you who can split your check into multiple accounts, you may want to automate the funding process. Sending a set amount of money per paycheck to the Emergency Account is a great idea that should be considered.

In order to properly figure out how much money should be designated, you must make it all the way through Chapter 5. You must figure out how much money is getting deposited into the Spending Account. At that point you can figure out how much you want to allow for your spending and how much you want to designate for the Emergency Account.

Once you figure out how much money should be pulled per paycheck, get with your payroll office and set up direct deposit. But don't do this until you have your Payments Account up and running, and that includes having enough cash to cover one month ahead of your bills.

The idea of an Emergency Account is that it's locked up, but also accessible. You don't want to put your Emergency Account in a CD (Certificate of Deposit), for example, because you wouldn't be able to access it easily. But you don't want to have your Emergency Account so available that you can use it without thinking. It takes some discipline to fund an Emergency Account and keep it at your target balance, but we're confident you'll be happy with the results.

CASE STUDY: Andrew and Natalie go from Disorganized to Organized

Andrew and Natalie had a very nice income, but had nothing to show for it. They literally had hundreds of transactions a week from a stop at a grocery store to a rent house mortgage, all the way to their water bill from their personal residence, and everything in between. I felt stressed too when I was helping get them organized because I couldn't keep track of everything. They needed a system that helped manage their personal lives and their successful rental property business.

The problem Andrew and Natalie had was that they were spending the leftover money (rent payment minus mortgage payment) when the rent was paid, and they were not prepared when a big bill would come in for a water heater or faucet that was leaking. They were always flying by the seat of their pants. With a little vision and planning, we created a system for them that would simplify their lives and create clarity and control.

Step One was to open an account that only rent/mortgage payments would be run out of. Rent payments all come in during the first week of the month, and when they arrive Natalie deposits them into this account. For those of you who do have rental houses, what happens when they are vacant, for example, when a renter moves out and you are trying to rent it again? Does the mortgage stop? No, it doesn't. You still have to pay the mortgage. Will you be prepared for vacancy? Hopefully, but if not, there was a *critical* step that we suggested they consider.

We wanted them to front this account with a month of mortgage payments (for a total of $3,000 approximately) to cover all the mortgage payments for a month, should the houses become vacant for a month. The odds that all three would be vacant at the same time is unlikely but not impossible. If that should occur, they will be prepared. Remember our sentence from earlier in the book: Be intentional, be pro-active and be patient. Andrew and Natalie picked up some extra hours at work and cut back lifestyle for four months until they accomplished this goal. Any repairs that needed to take place on any of their rent houses would now come out of this account. The mortgage payments were set to be automatically withdrawn from this account as well. If there were no repairs, money stayed in this account and continued to grow, getting them that much further ahead.

Step Two was to create some clarity and control for their personal residence. Now that rent income and company paychecks were being kept separate, we could shift focus and create a system that would help control their spending and make the difficult task of paying their bills fast and efficient. We set up a Payments Account and figured out how much money it took to run their household for the month ($3,750). They decided to feed the Payments Account with $4,000 a month, and it would be funded based on each of their pay cycles. Andrew and Natalie each get paid once a month, so they each funded $2,000 per paycheck. They deposited the remaining money into their Spending Account, and they now knew *exactly* how much money they had left to enjoy life as they chose. As stated earlier, they did not have any money to their name when we discussed this plan, so in order to save one month of bills for this account, they again worked extra in order to complete this step as taught.

We then looked at the Emergency Account and discussed how much money they felt comfortable with. They wanted to have a good cushion (six months of savings) in case something catastrophic happened and one of them lost their job for whatever reason. They are not at that point yet, but will get there eventually. It may take them two years of monthly contributions to get the Emergency Account to the balance they want, but with hard work and patience, I believe it will happen.

Put yourself in their shoes for a second, and pretend that everything is properly funded and things are running smoothly. Can you feel the peace that they have in their household? Their Money Funnel System is working like a well-oiled machine.

Giving families peace, clarity and control is our goal for every Money Funnel System that we have helped create. Are there others that are yet to be discovered? Absolutely! Who knows, Andrew and Natalie may change theirs and modify some things later down the road. The foundation is built, the system is running, and can and should be changed with time if they feel it is necessary.

CHAPTER 6

The Spending Account

We get it. Who actually really likes to *save* money? We see something we want, and we spend money on it. But how would it feel if you didn't have to worry, even the littlest of bits, when you went to spend money on a new pair of shoes or some new clothes for the kids?

Income Stream

Emergency Account

Spending Account

Payments Account

Lots of people we have met ask us to give them tips on how to control their spending. Why do they ask us this question? If they weren't accidentally spending their bills money, why would they worry? Maybe they sincerely do want to control how much money they spend, and that's great. But for most others, they spend too much money and put themselves in a bind. They are losing the race and can't catch their competition.

The Spending Account is what you get to do with the balance of your paycheck. Spending without worry is the reward you get to give yourself every month that you're using the Money Funnel System effectively.

Remember, the accounts shown in the illustration are the essential accounts needed to run the basic Money Funnel System. You may decide to have more to be able to manage your money effectively. After you have properly funded your Payments Account and have your Emergency Account set up with a way to fund it to its target, then you get to set up—and use—the Spending Account.

With that being said, let's dive into the Spending Account and explain what the function of this account is.

Account Specifics

First of all, let us first remind you of something very important. Once you have completed all the steps in Chapter 4, your allocated bills money has already been deposited into your Payments Account. That money is gone, you don't even see it. The only money you should see in your Spending Account is what is left over.

Some people have it backwards. They spend money on themselves before they take care of their household. We used to be like this. This is why we believe in the Money Funnel System and what it does for you and your household. It takes away the ease and accessibility to your money and thus the temptation to spend too much money.

The Money Funnel System teaches to take care of your household first and then save money for an emergency. Then you know how much is left, and you can spend that without heartache or worry. But always, *spending is secondary to household responsibilities!*

We stated this earlier, but it's important to stress the point again. Those readers who don't have access to direct deposit or can't split their check into multiple accounts, it's going to be important to remove the funds for your payment and emergency accounts before you can get your hands on it. Withdraw the money from the Spending Account and deposit it into the Payments Account as soon as possible.

Account Activity

In the Payments Account, there are very specific transactions that we want you to consider and account for on a monthly basis. The activity in the Payments Account is sporadic, planned, and must be kept an eye on to ensure it's running properly. The Spending Account, on the other hand, is not nearly as strict. There is definitely more flexibility in this account.

Technically speaking, this account balance could go down to $0.05 (or even $0.00) and you would still be okay as long as you knew it was to be replenished the next pay cycle. Do we recommend this? No! But hypothetically speaking, you could spend almost all the money in this account and be okay. Why? You will *have not* spent your bills money.

Instant Balance Check

Pull out your smartphone or go online and look at your account balance on your checking account. Ask yourself the following question. "Can I spend every last penny in this account and be okay?" Most of the time the answer is no. If you do spend every last penny in your checking account, you may have spent money designated for your car payment or mortgage.

Are you tired of constantly having to do mental math in your head? You may look at your account balance and see $5,000 in there. You think, "Yay! Spend away!" But do you really have $5,000 to spend when $3,000 of that is designated for bills? If you have your Payments Account set up, you know that you have $2,000 to spend. That's when you can "spend away" without penalty, unless of course you overspend and overdraw the account. As the month continues, you are spending away and depleting the account balance. You must keep a constant eye on this account.

This account can get away from you, especially if you walk into your favorite store. We often joke that when we visit our favorite big box store, somehow things just jump off the shelves and land in the cart. It's amazing! Then the next morning we have the inevitable financial hangover as we look at all the bags on the kitchen table. How many different wreaths do we need for the front door? Seriously.

Let's pretend you went on a family vacation and spent $1,500 over the weekend. If the account balance started with $2,000, you would only have $500 left in the account. You would know that you would have to be very mindful of how you spent the rest of that money. However, if you didn't have the Payments Account set up, you may try to kid yourself and say you had a starting *spending* balance of $5,000, and after your $1,500 weekend, you think, "I will have $3,500 in the account. I'll be fine." Then you go out and spend more money instead of paying bills. We would like to think that would never happen. But we did it. People tell us they do it. Surprisingly, it happens very often.

This is why the Money Funnel System is so effective. It's a *lot* harder to overspend when you know exactly how much you *can* spend and still have your bills taken care of.

Account Transactions

The purpose of this account is to run your "everyday" transactions that are going to take place. Below are some examples of the types of transactions that will take place out of this account:

- Lunch with coworkers
- Target run
- Date night
- Nail salon
- Weekend at the beach
- Movie night
- Night out with the girls
- Hunting with friends

The activity in this account is going to be all over the place. For us it is nearly impossible to keep track of every transaction. One night, as we were writing this book, my wife and I logged into our account and decided to count how many transactions took place out of this account in one month's time. We literally counted 116 transactions! If we didn't have our monthly payments handled in another account, this would be overwhelming to follow. One thing is for sure. We must constantly keep an eye on the balance in our Spending Account. Since implementing the Money Funnel System, we have yet to have an overdraft charge.

In our household we have two people, my wife and I, spending out of this account. It forces us to be in constant communication, which is actually good for a marriage.

The number one cause of divorce in North America is money fights and money problems. The Money Funnel System can help a husband and wife get on the same page and communicate about money.

Since Cristina stays home with the kids, she's usually out running all the errands during the day. We stay in constant communication. We call each other to confirm the bank balance and give each other the head's up when we're about to spend money, like on an unplanned trip to the favorite store or a splurge trip to the coffee shop. We are not asking each other for permission to spend the money, but simply just keeping each other informed. To some people this may seem silly or even odd, but this is just our way of maintaining good communication. It's better to have a relaxed chat about the money you have rather than a stressful discussion about the money you had—and spent when you shouldn't have!

Gas and Groceries

Out of the hundreds of transactions taking place, two transactions in particular must be carefully considered. First of all, you must always have a budget for groceries. Depending on the size of your family, this could easily be a huge transaction. In our household we run our groceries out of our Spending Account. Cristina is able to efficiently plan out the meals and will make one trip to the grocery store a week.

We have a friend who likes really fresh food and cooks all the time. She goes to the store about every other day. We know others who live farther away from a town center and have to buy their groceries in bulk and make that last over a longer period of time. Whatever the case may be, we are going to suggest coming up with a budget for groceries. You can do this based on how often your paycheck comes in, or you can put a lump sum for the entire month and stick to that.

Some may choose to run their groceries out of their Payments Account and look at this as a payment. Others have a grocery account specifically set up. That's fine as well.

Same goes for gas. This is another transaction that is constant, big, and must be paid. You can keep gas receipts for a month or two, and add them up and get an average monthly fuel expense. This can be your starting point for you to project how much money is needed for gas on a monthly basis. You can run these transactions out of your Spending Account, out of your Payments Account, or have the separate account set for gas and groceries. Do what works best, meaning do what allows you to keep track of your money the most effectively.

In our household we have a separate account that we run our gas and vehicle maintenance out of. Because we have a vehicle reimbursement program that my company uses, it's easier for us to run it in this manner. If my company closed down tomorrow and Cristina went back to teaching, we think we would consider running these two (gas and groceries) out of our Payments Account. In any case, those are just some things to consider.

Limit Your Spending

Let's go back to our hypothetical $5,000 per month total income. You designate $3,000 to your Payments Account. What do you do with the remaining $2,000? We recommend at the very least that you keep a minimum balance in the Spending Account.

If you choose to spend all $2,000, you won't be in a financial bind paying your bills. But what about emergencies?

In the previous chapter, we mentioned the importance of limiting your spending so you can send money to the Emergency Account until you achieve your desired balance.

Here's an example of what we mean. You have $2,000 deposited into the Spending Account. Your target Emergency Account balance is $6,000. Could you get by on spending a $1,000 a month for six months while you build up your Emergency Account? It might be tight and you can't go out to dinner and the movies—or buy the newest phone or a cool new pair of shoes. But you'll have money saved for when you need it.

If $1,000 isn't realistic, then what about $500? You would still have $1,500 a month, or $375 per week. At this rate ($500 per month) it would take you a year to build up to the $6,000 goal. You might find this is a doable target, one you can easily stick to.

Decide what you are trying to accomplish, and start working towards that. Once you have your Emergency Account in place, that is when you can decide what's next—buy a new car, reward yourself with a vacation, or enjoy an expensive dinner. Have a goal, limit your spending and watch as you begin accomplishing some financial goals you have set forth for yourself.

What If You Don't Have a Computer, Smartphone, or Tablet

It may be hard for some to believe, but there are people who don't own or don't know how to use modern technology. The Money Funnel System runs much more efficiently if you have a computer, tablet or smartphone to check balances and move money around as needed. There are still many people out there though who like to put the pen to paper and keep hard money on their person. However, if you're really good about recording transactions and can be disciplined enough to physically move money from bank to bank, you can still implement the Money Funnel System organizational concept.

You will not benefit from the efficiency of it, but you will still gain some control through the organization of your money. Keeping up with the three foundational accounts is still possible with paper statements and written tracking of your spending.

If what you're already doing with your money is working, don't completely scrap it. But if it isn't working, then it's time to change. Take a look at your situation, and decide what's best for you.

Spending Account as its Designated

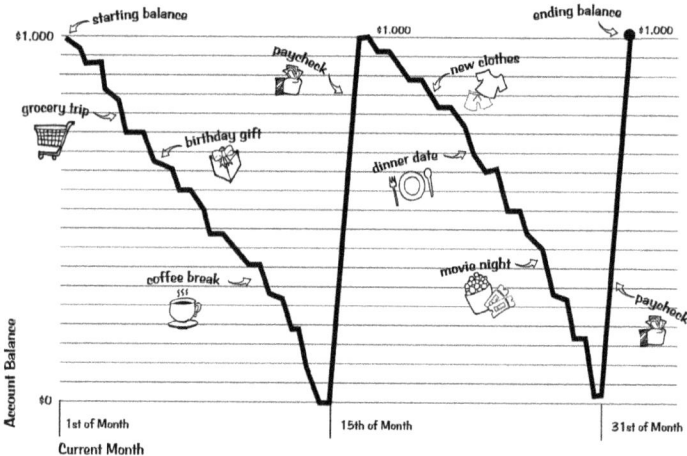

Now that you understand what this account is designed for, let's take a look at the graph and discuss a few points. We're going to use the hypothetical $2,000 per month for spending. The person in the example gets paid twice a month, so he must ration this money to last for one-half of a month. Someone who gets multiple paychecks during the month will have spikes in the balance sprinkled in as their paychecks arrive.

In any case, the money in this account is constantly creeping towards $0.00. Hopefully you don't ever get close to that amount, but it could.

We never feel bad about spending money in this account. We want to enjoy our money, and you should too. Especially when we go out of town or on a vacation, we don't think twice. Again, we are responsible and have already taken care of our household.

Our money doesn't control us. We control it, and the benefit of knowing that with certainty is, as the commercial says, priceless.

CASE STUDY: David and Linda Don't Trust Each Other With Money

David and Linda have been married for twenty years, and they choose not to combine their finances. Although we would highly recommend combining your finances, we wanted to show that the Money Funnel System can still work in a household situation like this.

David is responsible for paying the mortgage, and Linda is responsible for paying water, electricity, cable, and internet. They choose to run their grocery bill out of the Payments Account as well and split that equally. In running through their numbers, David sends $1,200 per month for the mortgage and $300 a month for food for a total monthly deposit of $1,500. Linda sends a total of $700 for utilities and $300 a month for food for a total monthly deposit of $1,000. David gets paid twice a month (on the 1st and the 15th), so he sends two deposits of $750 per paycheck to equal his $1,500 to the household Payments Account, and deposits the rest of his paycheck into his Spending Account. What he chooses to do with that money is up to him. He has fulfilled his obligation to the household. Linda gets paid every Friday, so she sends $250 per paycheck to the household Payments Account, and the rest of her check goes to her Spending Account.

They have also agreed that Linda can withdraw the money on those "magic months" where she gets an extra paycheck. The household Payments Account is non-negotiable and that money can't be touched for any reason. David and Linda fortunately had some savings, so they each took $750 from their savings account (for a total starting balance of $1,500) and opened their household Payments Account. They are not fully one month ahead of their bills, but this will work for them based on the dates their bills are getting drafted. Linda has chosen to monitor the activity in the account once a month, just to make sure everything is running smoothly. When it comes to buying groceries, they agreed to look at the receipt together and make sure they didn't spend more than what was budgeted.

The best part of this system for this couple is that David and Linda can't spend their bills money. Each one now feels the other is being responsible for holding up their end of the bargain. We checked back with them after some time, and they were now throwing around the idea of combining their finances. Maybe they will get there one day, as the Money Funnel System has helped them to build trust with one another. Trust is a foundational part of marriage, and if the Money Funnel System can help strengthen that bond, then it truly is a beautiful thing.

CHAPTER 7

Allocating Your Funds

This is a recap of how to fund your accounts. You now know the how's and why's of each account, and we have talked about the importance of allocating your funds into the foundational three accounts. Or more, if that's how you want to set up your Money Funnel System.

Step One of the Payments Account was all about figuring out how much income you earn every month. This is how much money is coming into your money funnel. In that step we had you pull out your pay stubs and estimate what your total monthly income is. In this step we need to figure out how often those paychecks are coming in so we can designate a certain amount to be sent to your three accounts.

This step is very important because you can encounter overdraft fees over time if your payments and Spending Accounts are not properly funded.

This step can be easy for some, while for others it's going to be more challenging. We came up with an easy formula to help you quickly navigate this step. We also have some examples for you to read through that can help you understand what we are trying to accomplish.

Many companies offer direct deposit, which is by far the most efficient way to instantly get your paycheck. Some companies still hand out paper checks. There are others that pay in cash.

Additionally, frequency of paychecks is different across every company or business. I have had jobs in the past that pay once a month, twice a month (on the 1st and the 15th), bi-weekly (every other Friday), and weekly (every Friday). Depending on the frequency of your paycheck, you will need to calculate how much money should be designated out of each paycheck to be deposited into your three foundational accounts.

If you have a job that pays you in cash, then you are going to have to be more disciplined and deposit the money where it needs to go before you have the chance to spend it. Having that cash in hand will make it easier to spend so be intentional and deposit it into the Payments Account as quickly as possible.

To find out how much money to designate per paycheck for your Payments Account, use the formula below.

$$\frac{\textit{Payments Account Total}}{\textit{Number of Paychecks}} = \textbf{Amount per Paycheck}$$

Once you have the total amount per paycheck, you can figure out how much money you need to designate per paycheck to properly fund your accounts.

Because the Payments Account is most important, we're going to concentrate on that first.

Let's run through an example of Jane who is trying to figure out how much money per paycheck should be designated to properly fund her Payments Account.

1. Jane has figured out that she needs $2,000 per month in her Payments Account.

   a. If she got paid once a month: She would deposit a lump sum of $2,000

$$\frac{\textit{\$2,000}}{\textit{1 Paycheck per month}} = \textbf{\$2,000 / check}$$

b. If she got paid twice a month: She would deposit $1,000 per paycheck ($1,000 x 2 = $2,000)

$$\frac{\$2,000}{2 \ Paychecks \ per \ month} = \mathbf{\$1,000 \ / \ check}$$

c. If she got paid bi-weekly: She would still deposit $1,000 per paycheck.

   i. In this case, there are "magic months" that Jane will get 3 paychecks. Some months $3,000 would get deposited (an extra $1,000) to the Payments Account. We recommend "worst case scenario" and will keep this number at 2 paychecks per month.

$$\frac{\$2,000}{2 \ Paychecks \ per \ month} = \mathbf{\$1,000 \ / \ check}$$

d. If she got paid weekly: She would deposit $500 per paycheck.

   i. In this case as well, there are "magic months" where Jane will get 5 paychecks. Some months $2,500 would get deposited (an extra $500) to the Payments Account. Again, we recommend "worst case scenario" and will keep this number at 4 paychecks per month.

$$\frac{\$2,000}{4 \ Paychecks \ per \ month} = \mathbf{\$500 \ / \ check}$$

If by the end of the year, you have accrued quite a bit of extra cushion in your account, you could always withdraw that extra money and apply it to debt. Of course, the choice is yours.

It gets really tricky when you are married and have multiple paychecks coming in at different times. This only has to be done this way if the couple is combining their finances.

Let's run through an example of Robert and Andrea who are trying to figure out how much money per paycheck should be designated to properly fund their Payments Account. If they were to keep their finances separate, the example we just discussed above will work for each of them individually. In this case, they are combining their finances and the same formula used above still works.

1. Robert and Andrea have figured out they need $3,000 to cover their Payments Account. Robert gets paid bi-weekly and Andrea gets paid every month. Some months they have three paychecks coming in (two from Robert and one from Andrea) and on their "magic months" they have four (three from Robert and one from Andrea). We are going to go with a worst-case scenario, and assume three paychecks a month.

That turns out to be $2,000 per month for Robert, and $1,000 per month from Andrea for a total Payments Account goal of $3,000.

$$\frac{\$3,000}{3\ Paychecks\ per\ month} = \$1,000 / \text{check}$$

Let's also run through Charles and Megan's numbers, who are also trying to figure out how to properly fund their Payments Account.

2. Charles and Megan also are married and have figured out they need $3,600 to fund their Payments Account. Charles gets paid once a week, and Megan gets paid twice a month. Some months they have six checks (four from Charles and two from Megan), while other months they have seven checks (five from Charles and two from Megan). We are going to go with a worst-case scenario and assume six paychecks a month.

That turns out to be $2,400 per month for Charles, and $1,200 per month from Megan for a total Payments Account goal of $3,600.

$$\frac{\$3,600}{6\ Paychecks\ per\ month} = \textbf{\$600 / check}$$

Feel free to modify as you feel is best, it really doesn't matter. Some couples may choose to put one hundred percent of their spouses' paycheck away (which is what we did for a while). More power to you! As long as by the end of the month you deposit what is required for your Payments Account, anything above that is gravy on the biscuit.

Now all of the "set up" is complete. Next is the fun part. Get with your payroll, set up your direct deposit, and start feeding the Payments Account.

Once you have your Payments Account funded, and you are using it religiously every month, then you can set up the Emergency Account. We've already discussed how to fund this. Take what's left from your paychecks, and decide how much you need to designate for the Emergency Account. Get your Emergency Account built to your target balance, and then you can either continue to save or designate that money into the Spending Account.

The Spending Account is the last account to be funded, but the money is there for you to *spend*. Enjoy it. You've earned it.

Funneling Your Check

Once you have figured out how much money you need to allocate into each account, it's time to put the plan into action. There are going to be several situations that you may encounter depending on your employer and what restrictions may exist.

Let's start with those who have direct deposit available. You first need to ask if you are able to split your check into multiple accounts. If you are only able to send one hundred percent of your paycheck to only one account, then this step will need to be modified. If this is the case, you are going to physically withdraw/deposit the proper amount in your Payments Account. You may need to do this multiple times a month, depending on your pay cycle. This will definitely be more work, but worth it if that's your only option. Not removing the money and having access to it can turn into a bigger problem, as we explained before.

If you are able to split your check up, then we suggest you take advantage of this option. Some companies allow you to do this as many times as you would like. We actually split my check into four unequal parts. This is by far the most efficient way of keeping your Money Funnel System running smoothly. It of course takes careful planning, but being able to automatically fund your Payments Account, and any other accounts you have set up, is such a blessing.

Remember, once your household is taken care of, it's up to you to decide how much you want to save versus spend. Once that system is drawn out and fully implemented, then you can split your income up accordingly based on that. If you are just starting and don't have multiple accounts, then just split your check in two. Send the proper amount to your Payments Account, and the remaining will go to your Spending Account.

The following page shows an example of a Direct Deposit Authorization form that would need to be filled out and given to your payroll office. This is just one example, but every employer is unique and may require something different.

Direct Deposit Authorization

I authorize _____ to send credit entries, as well as appropriate
Adjustments and debit entries to my/our accounts as indicated below.

Account #1

Account Type: _____ Checking _____ Savings
Institution Name: _____
Bank Routing #/ ABA #: _____ Account #: _____
Percentage to be deposited into this account: _____

Account #2

Account Type: _____ Checking _____ Savings
Institution Name: _____
Bank Routing #/ ABA #: _____ Account #: _____
Percentage to be deposited into this account: _____

Please attach a voided check for each account here

_____   _____
Signature   Date

_____
Printed Name

It may take a pay cycle for the process to actually kick in. For those of you who get paid once a month, it will take longer to start the funding process. That's okay. Be patient.

Another situation you may need to be patient with is if you don't have access to direct deposit through your employer. In this case, you will need to physically deposit the budgeted amount into the account.

Now your Payments Account is set to be consistently funded. Breathe a sigh of relief. You did it. It's time to begin tracking the activity in a spreadsheet.

We know that setting up the Money Funnel System takes some work and dedication, but it's something that you never have to do from scratch again. If your circumstances change, then you will need to be sure and make the necessary funding adjustment.

Track and Watch

The worst thing that you can do is to have this system up and running and then forget about it. What if you budgeted $150.00 for electricity and you have a bill of $225? If you are not monitoring as the money gets taken out, you may miss a bill that was higher than expected. You have to keep an eye on the account from time to time. We go into our Payments Account twice a month and look at the activity. We also take the time to fill out our "actual payments" column with what the bill actually was.

Here's a blank version of the spreadsheet again, so you can use it to start your own Money Funnel System. The Excel® spreadsheet is available to download at www.themoneyfunnelsystem.com. Enter promo code MFSHEETS to receive your free copy.

Bill Name	Month 1			
	Projected	Actual	Difference	Bill Due Date
Total	$ -	$ -	$ -	

CASE STUDY: Dan Gets Control of his Spending

I met Dan while he was at work, and I caught him at the right time in his life. I was returning an item, and after we were done with the transaction, I felt compelled to talk money and financial organization with him. At the time of our discussion, he was struggling to pay his bills and was constantly stressing about money. In the earlier section of the book called "The Race," this is exactly what Dan was struggling with. He couldn't get paid fast enough. He was constantly waiting for that next paycheck to get deposited.

He had lots of bills that were due on the 7th and 10th of the month and his paycheck didn't come in until the 15th. He felt like he was always behind and was struggling. On top of that, he was running his household out of one account so he was also spending money on groceries, gas, going out to eat, etc. He had no idea where his money was going. When I explained how we could to set up a system that would alleviate his stress, he was ready to listen.

I told him to write down every single bill that he needs to pay (over-estimating slightly) that it takes to run his household, just as we teach in the book ($2,700 in his case). Once he came up with a grand total, we told him the key to making this system work was to place one month of bills as a starting balance to his Payments Account. We told him, "If we can figure out how to put $2,700 in the Payments Account now, the stress of paying your bills for this month is gone! Now your next paycheck that comes in will start funding next month's bills, and you now will be one month ahead."

Fortunately for Dan, he had company stocks that he stated he could cash out to start his Payments Account. Now his bills would be separate from his spending, and now we could create a secondary goal for what's left in his Spending Account. He wanted to pay off some credit cards, so that's exactly what he did.

We kept going into the store periodically to check on Dan, and every time we talked, he was excited and his stress going down. When we sat down again, he was able to send $850 per month to pay off credit cards. That's what was left after sending $2,700 to the Payments Account and leaving himself $2,000 for spending. Remember, by his paying off his credit cards and no longer having that bill, he now had a choice. He could send less money to his Payments Account, or he could keep sending the same amount and make the account grow even more. He chose to keep sending the same amount, and let the Payments Account build up even more and be even further ahead of his bills.

Additionally, for Dan, he also got something out of the system that we have not discussed up to this point, and I wanted to give him credit for this. He stated, "When only my bills were coming out of my Payments Account, I could actually see how much I was paying for each bill. So I have now made a goal of trying to reduce each bill as much as possible, so I can be even further ahead." This statement is so true. When you run your bills/spending out of the same account, your bills and how much you are actually paying can get lost in all the transactions. You may forget how much you are paying for cable. Maybe you can negotiate a deal and shop around a little. That doesn't hurt at all.

Make the Surplus Work for You

The Money Funnel System is remarkably simple to run if it is properly set up and consistently funded every month. We no longer worry about getting our bills paid. We know how much money we can spend every month, and we make sure we have extra for rainy days and holidays.

In short, we are in control of our money, and there's nothing like that feeling.

And, we also know because we have taught ourselves to be disciplined with our money that we are building a surplus. We're still fairly young, but we know that we will one day be able to retire. Our kids will be grown and out of the house. We will have saved for their college, and we will also have money to retire on and to live the life we want in our golden years.

Money is something that must be managed no matter how old, young, or in between you are.

The way we have our Money Funnel System set up automatically creates a surplus, and because that surplus is building every month, we've decided our next step is figuring out the best way to make that money work for us.

We're not financial planners. We're not licensed to sell any type of financial services product or insurance.

However, we know that if we do not manage our surplus well, we will spend it. After all the hard work we've put into ensuring our Money Funnel System works for us and our finances, we don't want that to happen. We've been studying up on what we can do, and we want to give you a list of books we've found helpful. These various systems help you turn your surplus cash potentially into financial independence when you need it later in life. Our goal is to have the freedom to work because we want to not because we need to.

Here's what we have found informative:

Getting Out of Debt:
The Total Money Makeover, Dave Ramsey
Financial Peace University, Dave Ramsey

The Envelope System:
Dave Ramsey's tools and materials available on his website www.daveramsey.com.

Retire Inspired, Chris Hogan
Everyday Millionaires, Chris Hogan

The Millionaire Next Door, Thomas J. Stanley, Ph.D. & William D. Danko, Ph.D.

Richer Than a Millionaire ~ A Pathway to True Prosperity, William D. Danko, Ph.D. & Richard J. Van Ness, Ph.D.

JAIME and CRISTINA—Our Customized Money Funnel System

This is what our Money Funnel System looks like today; however, it didn't always look like this. Just recently our Money Funnel System was modified because Cristina quit her job to take care of our kids full time. It will eventually change again, as do all things in life.

Because of this change in income, we opened a separate account and called it the Business Expenses Account. I recently started buying and selling things on eBay so I wanted to run purchases out of

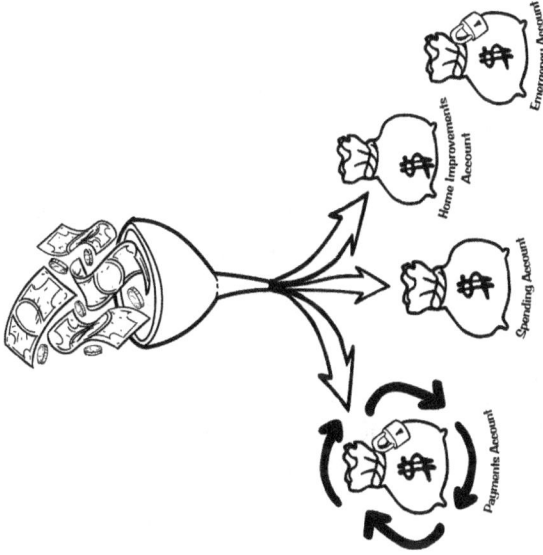

Business Income → Business Expenses

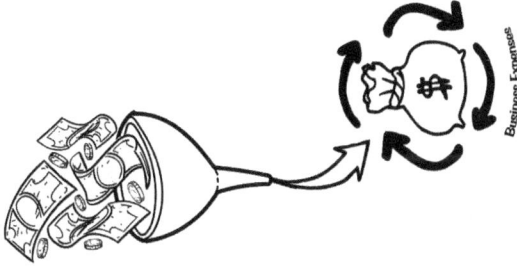

Income Stream → Home Improvements Account, Emergency Account, Spending Account, Payments Account

Vehicle Reimbursement Check → Vehicle Maintenance Account

its own account. The activity in the Business Expenses Account is all over the place. I am constantly buying things, selling them and such is the cycle. The main advantage of this account is that at the end of the month I can see how much profit is left. The starting balance was $1,000 and periodically I withdraw the profits and deposit them into the Spending Account. This account is also at a separate bank, so withdrawing the money and depositing into the Spending Account must be done manually. Additionally, I am sending $75 per paycheck (direct deposit) into this account. This bank required at least $300 per month be deposited (via direct deposit) in order to avoid a fee.

Next, we have our Emergency Account which is untouchable, until we have an emergency. We stated earlier that our account took a hit because our son Isaiah broke his arm. This is a savings account which we are currently in the process of refilling back to our target balance of $12,000. Once we get to this target balance, we will be on the six months side of household expenses. Because of the scar of having been laid off, we want to have that cushion should that situation arise again.

Another account we run is our Home Improvements Account. This is the last account that gets any money. Only when we have our Emergency Account refilled does any remaining money get deposited into this account. We live in an older home and enjoy doing updates here and there. This is a small pool of money we keep should we have the time to tackle a project.

We have already taught you what the Spending Account is for. This is where we run our groceries, eating out, date nights, shopping, coffee runs and all other random, and typically casual, charges. We average around a hundred transactions a month, and this account is by far the account we pay the most attention to. We run two debit cards out of this account, one for each of us. We have spent the balance all the way down to $5, but didn't break a sweat. When we keep within the boundaries of the Money Funnel System, we can enjoy some of our income and spend guilt-free because our payments are taken care of.

Our Payments Account is next and is by far the most important account. I am depositing $475 per week, via direct deposit, to this account. This takes care of the household for the entire month ($475 x 4 = $1,900). Our Payments Account includes electricity, cell phone, cable, health insurance, educational savings accounts (ESA's), water and life insurance. Additionally, this includes the savings aspect of this account. We budget for taxes ($1,500 paid at the end of the year), home insurance ($700/year) and car insurance ($600 every 6-months). Because my paycheck comes every Friday, we have "magic weeks" in which I get an extra paycheck. Some months have five Fridays. We still feed the account with that extra $475, but don't withdraw the money. We started with one month of bills as our starting balance, and it has grown to be two months ahead. Fast forward two years, we may be 4 or 5 months ahead of our payments!

The last account we have set up is the Vehicle Maintenance Account. I run all of my work expenses out of this account, and includes purchasing gas. I spend at least $450 per month on gas, and get an oil change at least every two months. Because we get a lump sum reimbursement on the fifteenth of every month, it made sense to run all these expenses out of its own account. If I ever lost my job, this account would go away. I also have the truck payment drafted from this account as well. I am currently funding it (via direct deposit) with $30 per paycheck. Additionally, I got a second debit card so Cristina runs her gas out of this account as well.

Hypothetically, we could go out with the family and fill up with gas, go out to eat, and while out buy some things to sell. In that instance, I would pull out three different debit cards and take care of each transaction.

Looks like too much work? Looks complicated? Trust us, it's not. It works like a well-oiled machine with every transaction coming out of its proper account. We wouldn't have it any other way.

The Money Funnel System offers anyone who implements the steps as we teach them a level of financial stability that many people think is unattainable.

Anyone can use this system. No matter how much money you make or what financial background you are coming from, this will help you gain control of your finances—and stay there.

www.ingramcontent.com/pod-product-compliance
Lightning Source LLC
Chambersburg PA
CBHW071437210326
41597CB00020B/3838